OTHER BOOKS BY R. THOMAS BURGER

Auburn Murder Stories
with Sergeant Joseph DiVietro

Each chapter outlines a true murder that occurred in Auburn. It contains many original Police reports, photos, diagrams, wanted posters and other items that haven't been seen in years - many printed here for the first time. *24 stories.*

It Happened in Auburn

A collection of short stories of Auburn's heroes, villains, cops and firemen, welcome home celebrations and funerals, strife and buildings that once were. All these stories occurred in Auburn. All were once on the "front page." *28 stories.*

ALONG THESE STREETS AND ROADS

Stories from Auburn and Cayuga County

R. THOMAS BURGER

Auburn, NY

Copyright © 2014 by R. Thomas Burger.

All rights reserved. No part of this book may be used or reproduced in any manner whatsoever without written permission except in the case of brief quotations embodied in critical articles and reviews.

Cover designed by R. Thomas Burger.

For information on this title contact:
Downtown Books Publishing
66 Genesee Street
Auburn, NY 13021
www.downtownbooksandcoffee.com

ISBN: 978-0-69273-395-0

For my wife Cathy, my "Little Gi"
...forever loved, forever missed.

TABLE OF CONTENTS

A Beginning ix

Writing a Book 1

Peter H. Myers' *Ensenore* & George Clark 9

Train Crash Kills Four 15

Edwin L. Thornton, Thorngreen and Mercy Hospital 23

George F. Wills 27

Albert H. Hamilton: Forensic Expert or Charlatan 31

Brewing in the Prison City 39

Farm Equipment and Wagons 45

Rail City 49

General Clinton D. Macdougall 55

West Side Murders and Hauntings 59

The Union Army Fights in Auburn 67

A Niles Murder Mystery 75

A Murder in Weedsport 83

Oliver Curtis Perry "The Lone Wolf Bandit" 89

The Sheldon Case 99

Annie Edson Taylor Niagara Falls Daredevil 105

Herman Bartels Sr. and the Old Fanning Brewing Co. ... 111

Frontenac Burns, Eight Die 119

George E. Carr 127

A Horse Thief, A Car Thief and a Daring Jail Escape 131

Bandit's Robbery Goes Wrong 137

Murder in Cayuga 141

Mysterious Blast Blows Local Home Apart 157

Cayuga County's Gangster Deputy Sheriff 165

We Have Found Our New Home 169

Robbery Suspects Apprehended Quickly 173

They Were Heroes 177

One Tenant Dies as Auburn Hotel Fire Destroys Landmark 185

A BEGINNING
Auburn and Cayuga County

As the American Revolutionary War began, the struggling American Army needed men to fight. To entice men to enlist and serve New York State promised them farm land in the vast unknown western "frontier" of the State for their service after the war. This land, commonly called "The Military Tract," was occupied by the Cayuga and Seneca Indians. After the newly formed United States successfully gained their freedom from Great Britain the State of New York bought up the Indian lands and military survivors began dividing up the territory into lots for the soldiers who had served.

Soon the new settlers began arriving and small hamlets and villages began developing throughout the county. There was Weed's Basin (Weedsport), Jakway's Corners (Cato), Milton (Genoa), Owasco Flats (Moravia), Bucksville (Port Byron) and Hardenburg's Corners (Auburn).

Cayuga County was formed in 1799 from land once part of Onondaga County. Later the Counties of Seneca and Tompkins were formed from parts of Cayuga County. At the court house in Aurora, on May 28, 1799, a County government was formed. At that time Aurora was the county seat. It wasn't until 1805 that Auburn, probably because of its central location in the County, became the County seat.

Over the many years since these early times Cayuga County and the City of Auburn have grown. Being centrally located in the State the Old Genesee Turnpike, The Erie Canal and the railroads brought more people to the area. The City of Auburn became an industrial city and at one time was larger than the cities of Syracuse and Rochester. Many county and city residents became quite successful as inventors, poets, authors, painters and in industry, government, medicine and the law. The names of Fillmore, Seward, Tubman,

Rockefeller and Howland to today's TV star John Walsh and NASCAR star Regan Smith are only a few of our many celebrated residents.

The short stories retold in this book will not only cover a variety of subjects from daring train robberies and wrecks, murders and jail breaks, disastrous fatal fires but also some of the men, whether they were good or bad, that lived and died in Cayuga County and Auburn. It's a journey back in time that's well worth taking!

ALONG THESE STREETS AND ROADS

Stories from Auburn and Cayuga County

WRITING A BOOK

Since writing *"Auburn Murder Stories"* and *"It Happened in Auburn,"* I've learned a couple of things about writing a book...

The first is that researching the material and subjects for a book can be fun but can also be very frustrating. I rely heavily on old books and newspaper articles and you'd think, since most were written when the event occurred, that they'd be pretty accurate. However, I've found different spellings for people's names, that locations change and a particular annoyance is when different ages and dates of birth and death are listed. I could write another whole paragraph of examples, but I won't. I do the best that I can to ensure that most of the information is correct but from time to time even I find mistakes. So, please forgive me!

The second thing I've learned is that after you've completed the project, checked it (and I mean read and re-read hundreds of times, until you can't read it again) and its been published and on the shelves for sale you always seem to find a few misspelled words or a missing period or comma. However, even more frustrating is finding more information and photos about the subject matter. It sure would have been nice to include some of the "new" information and photos in the original book. Sometimes, however, it wouldn't have mattered as you run out of space and or the "new" material would inflate the cost to more than you desire.

Therefore, the following few pages will be devoted to adding some information and photos to a few of the stories in my two previously mentioned books...

R. THOMAS BURGER

VAN NEST MURDERS
(from *Auburn Murder Stories*)

On Thursday March 12, 1846, William Freeman, a poor African-American, murdered five persons in the town of Fleming. At that time most newspapers did not use actual photographs so they employed artists to draw sketches of the accused, victims and even crime scenes. These sketches were then drawn in local newspapers at the time of the murders and trial.

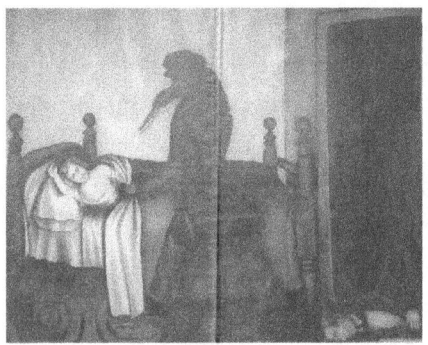

THE KELLER FAMILY
(from *Auburn Murder Stories*)

On a Thursday evening back in 1893, Mary Keller shot and killed her husband Emil, their nine month old daughter Anna and then herself. The three were buried together in a specially made coffin. Although somewhat uncommon today, years ago many people took photographs of their deceased loved ones. This photo of the family laid out in their specially made coffin was taken at the Gross Funeral Parlor.

PAULINA FROITZHEIM

(from *Auburn Murder Stories*)

In January 1884, Joseph Petmeky was convicted of murdering Pauline Froitzheim. He was sentenced to death and hung in the courtyard of the County Jail on Court Street, in Auburn on Thursday August 21, 1885.

On Thursday August 28, 1885, Joseph Petmeky's half brother Michael Wilbert, accompanied by prominent Auburnian Louis Newgass, a City Justice and expert examiner of the State Insurance Department, drove to St. Joseph's Cemetery and asked Cemetery Sexton Burns to exhume the body of his brother Joseph. Mr. Wilbert suspected foul play in that his brother's body had not been placed in his coffin. Sexton Burns informed the two men that an order to exhume the body would be required. Such order was then obtained from Cemetery Trustee John Lawler. When the coffin was exhumed the men found that its cover had been popped open due to the bloating of the body. Such a foul odor filled the air that the coffin and the remains of Petmeky were quickly reburied. Mr. Wilbert left satisfied that his brother's remains were properly buried at the cemetery.

JOSEPH PETMEKY,
THE YOUNG GERMAN WHO BUTCHERED MRS. FROITZHEIM, IN AUBURN, JUNE 1ST.

WELCOME HOME
(from *It Happened in Auburn*)

Myles Keogh was born in Leighlinbridge, Ireland on June 25, 1840. He had four brothers and eight sisters. After the start of the American Civil War in 1862, he left the Papal Army to enlist in the Union Army and was appointed to the rank of 2nd. Lieutenant. On June 25, 1876, he was killed while serving with Lt. Col. George Armstrong Custer, at the Battle of the Little Bighorn. At the time of the battle the deceased members of Custer's 7th. Cavalry were buried where they lay on the field. Captain Keogh had befriended the Martin family of Auburn and had requested their assistance to be buried in Auburn if he should be killed. On Friday October 26, 1877, he was buried in the Martin plot at Fort Hill Cemetery in Auburn.

The photos below show Capt. Keogh, his burial site on the battle field, his horse Comanche and his burial plot at Fort Hill. The marble cross at the foot of his stone was placed at the request of his sister in Ireland.

Little Bighorn burial site

Fort Hill burial site

R. THOMAS BURGER

BEHIND THE WALL

(from *It Happened in Auburn*)

On Wednesday morning August 6, 1890, William Kemmler became the first person in the world to be executed in an electric chair at Auburn Prison. He had killed his girlfriend Maditla "Tillie" Zeigler. The two had been living as husband and wife with Tillie's four year old daughter Ella, in Buffalo. Tillie had left her husband Fred, the father of her child, to run off with Kemmler. It was rumored that Fred "liked loose women," and Tillie could no longer put up with it. Her sister was married to Kemmler's brother Henry. On the morning of the murder Ella told Police "papa killed mama with a hatchet. He struck her on the head while she lay on the floor."

Kemmler was a hard drinker and believed Tillie was about to run off with one of his employees. After the murder his brother Henry and Tillie's father Frederick Tripner visited him in jail. When Mr. Tripner asked him why he killed Tillie, Kemmler replied "I had to. It's pretty bad, I know." Pressed for more information he refused to say anymore about the incident. His brother and Mr. Tripner made arrangements to have Tillie buried in Forest Lawn Cemetery, in Buffalo. They then took Ella back to Philadelphia and abandoned Kemmler.

Tilie & Ella as drawn in newspapers

While in prison Kemmler found religion and befriended the warden's wife. He wrote poetry and promised to write a poem about the electric chair. That never happened. Just before his execution he asked the warden's wife if he could wear a pretty star shaped pin she wore. When she offered him a prettier one he replied "No, I like that one. It reminds me of Heaven."

BEHIND THE WALL

(from *It Happened in Auburn*)

Many newspapers condemned the execution as "botched." Here is another drawing and the headlines printed in an "EXTRA" edition of the newspaper.

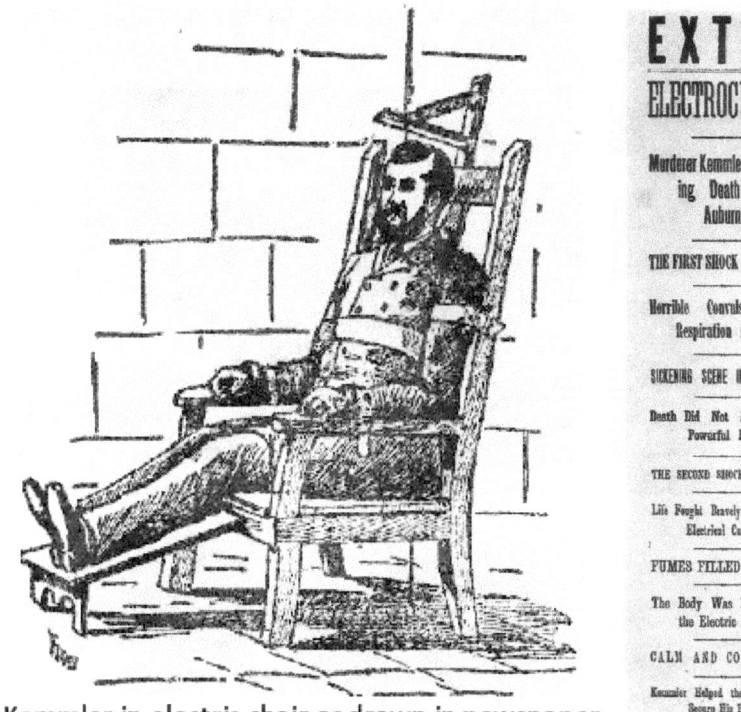

Kemmler in electric chair as drawn in newspaper

COON STREET EXPLOSION
(from *It Happened in Auburn*)

On Tuesday morning August 13, 1912, a terrible explosion destroyed the home of Raphael Cheche at 19 Coon Street (now Venice Street). The explosion killed his wife and three children and his friend Cosimo Carmelengo, of New Jersey. Here is another view of the destruction and the five hearse funeral precession making its way down Genesee Street to St. Francis Church.

PETER H. MYERS' *"ENSENORE"* & GEORGE CLARK

Peter Hamilton Myers was born in Herkimer, NY, on Tuesday August 4, 1812. At the age of 14, his brother Michael S. Myers, an Auburn attorney, brought him to Auburn and enrolled him in Dr. Rudd's school. He also attended an academy in Aurora, NY, until 1828. In 1829, his brother was appointed County Clerk and he made Peter his deputy. Peter continued his law studies and became a partner in the legal profession with his brother. They had offices in the newly built Beach Block, on Genesee Street (where Hislop's was located).

In 1848, Peter moved to Brooklyn and practiced law in New York City. In the late 1860s he returned to this area and resided in Skaneateles for a couple of years before settling again in Auburn in 1871. Peter was married to the former Margaret Swain, daughter of Captain William and Margaret Swain of 24 Grover Street. They had two children, a son William and a daughter Jessie.

During this time, Peter was quite an accomplished author. He wrote poems and American historical novels. Two of his earliest works were *"The First of the Knickerbockers"* and *"The Young Patron,"* both written in 1848. *"Bell Brundon"* and *"The Miser's Heir,"* were two of his prized tales that netted him $200.00 each from the Philadelphia Dollar Newspaper. He was also a regular contributor to the Knickerbocker Magazine. His last publication in verse, and perhaps his most famous piece, was *"Ensenore,"* in 1840.

Ensenore was the name given to the hero of the poem, a young frontiersman named after a friendly Virginia Indian Chief. In the poem Ensenore, who is familiar with war and Indian ways, pursues a band of Indians who had laid siege to his hometown, near Oriskany, and kidnapped his beloved Kathreen. He catches up to the Indians on the shores of Owasco Lake as they set up their summer camp and await the arrival of their Chief, Eagle Eye. Ensenore, disguised as a Narragansett sachem, is allowed into the Indian camp. Here he learns that the Indians' plan is to present Kathreen to their Chief for his pleasure. On the night of the Chief's arrival Ensenore escapes the Indian camp with Kathreen. Under the cover of darkness and a shower of arrows he rowed out onto Owasco Lake with the Indians in pursuit. He eludes them and returns home safely with Kathreen. The poem was so popular in the County that General William H. Seward sponsored its reprinting in 1875.

Peter Myers resided on South Street. He died of paralysis on Wednesday October 30, 1878, and is buried in Fort Hill Cemetery.

As all this was going on, Aaron Kellogg, of Moravia, was financing the building of a steamer he christened "Owasco," in 1847. The steamer sank on its maiden voyage and attempts to retrieve it failed. Meanwhile, Dr. Horatio Robinson and Benjamin B. Snow encouraged General Seward and Theodore Pomeroy to build two small cottages near theirs at Culver's Point, on the west side of the lake and a short distance above Cascade.

This beautiful area along the lake contained a water falls in a scenic glen with a post office and boat landing and could only be reached by boat or a ride along the Auburn-Moravia plank road.

It was here that Seward met an enterprising young man named George Clark. Clark had been born in Sullivan, Pa., on April 11, 1841. Shortly after his birth his parents moved to Sempronius. In 1863, Clark was living one mile west of Culver's Point with his wife Joanna. He began purchasing land all around Culver's Point where the proposed Southern Central Railroad was to be built over the old plank road from Auburn to Moravia. Clark was appointed station manager at Culver's Point and witnessed the first Southern Central train steaming along the tracks to Moravia on January 1, 1870.

In January 1874, Clark was appointed postmaster at Culver's Point. He also began building a large hall (100' x 28') close to the tracks on the south side of the glen. At that time, the reprinting of "Ensenore" was under way and it so inspired Clark that he named his new facility "Ensenore Glen." The picnic grounds and hall could accommodate up to 1,200 people and had boat rentals, croquet fields and swings. A favorite attraction was a walk up the glen to the falls. Clark had built a flight of stairs crossing the rivulet eight times before reaching the top for a spectacular view of the falls descending 437 feet as it made its way to the lake below. Grand opening ceremonies were held on June 10, 1874.

Clark's first year as station manager and businessman was so successful that he began building a four story hotel next to the hall and rail station. The hotel, named Ensenore Glen House opened in June of 1875. The beautiful 40 room hotel could accommodate 150 people. Each room had access to a broad veranda that encircled the hotel.

Clark, who had sponsored many boating and sculling races on the lake, sponsored what was considered one of the biggest scull racing events on September 27, 1877. Local Union Springs champion Charles Courtney went up against James Riley, of Saratoga, Nicholas Labergne, of Pittsburg and Frenchy Johnson, of Boston. Most businesses and schools closed for the day and a special 80 car train from Auburn to Ensenore was required to transport spectators. Close to 20,000 spectators watched as Courtney won the race.

To encourage people to visit Ensenore, Clark purchased Kellogg's steamer "Owasco." He repaired it and re-christened it "Ensenore." During launching ceremonies on Friday April 26, 1878, J. Lewis Grant, Esq., read the first few lines from Myers' poem Ensenore...

> *"To one of the fair lakes that lie*
> *Like mirrors 'neath a summer sky*
> *We welcome, as in days of yore*
> *Owasco's Chieftain----Ensenore"*

The steamer made daily trips up and down the lake taking its riders to all the popular lake venues and of course "Ensenore Glen." In 1884, Clark while still employed as the postmaster renamed the Culver's Point office Ensenore, the name it is still known as today and taken from Myers' poem of so long ago. George Clark, who contributed so much to the area, died on Wednesday November 28, 1906 and is buried at Indian Mound Cemetery in Moravia. He left a wife and two sons Frank and George. A third son named Seward, died at the age of 13 in 1889.

As some interesting side notes... In September 1894, George Clark was arrested for blowing off dynamite in the lake to kill fish. He paid a $100.00 fine. Wouldn't we like to know what was he thinking?

Michael S. Myers, Peter's older brother, was born at Waterford, NY, on April 15, 1801. He was educated in his hometown and read law there. In 1817 he entered the law office of Lockwood and Throop, in Auburn. He was admitted to the bar in 1825. Soon thereafter he moved to Aurora and practiced law there with the Honorable Glen Cuyler. In 1828, he was appointed County Clerk and returned to Auburn to reside. He appointed his brother Peter as his Deputy Clerk. He served nine years as Clerk and three years as District Attorney. In 1844, he was appointed Inspector of Prisons and in 1849 he was appointed postmaster of Auburn. He held many important offices and was active in public affairs. He died on Monday December 17, 1883 and is buried at Fort Hill Cemetery.

Charles E. Courtney was born in Union Springs on November 13, 1849. He was a skilled carpenter and a master oarsman who became a nationally known amateur champion sculler who never loss an amateur race. In 1877 he turned professional, a decision he always regretted. His controversial loss to Ned Hanlon was probably the reason for his retirement from professional racing. In 1883 he was appointed as head coach of Cornell University's rowing team. Under his direction the Cornell team won 14 of 24 varsity Intercollegiate Rowing Association Regattas. On June 12, 1915, while riding on a NY Central train and accompanying his Cornell team to another Intercollegiate Regatta, the train suddenly lurched forward and Courtney banged his head on a berth Even while bleeding from his nose and mouth he refused medical attention and continued on. On race day, the day after his accident, he was confined to bed. Upon returning to Ithaca he was diagnosed with a fractured skull. Since he only had a year left on his contract many thought he might retire. However, under doctor's care for several months he returned to his coaching duties and retired in 1920. Courtney died from apoplexy at his Cayuga Lake cottage at Farley's Point on July 17, 1920, not far from his boyhood home. He is buried at Lakeview Cemetery, in Cayuga, overlooking the lake he so much loved. His unique style of oaring became known as "Courtney's Stroke"---you always kept the back straight. He was quoted "No kinks in the back if I have anything to say about it."

Ensenore Glen House drawn newspaper ads

TRAIN CRASH KILLS FOUR

Tuesday September 26, 1899, was a cold drizzly morning when the west bound NY Central passenger train number 263 pulled out of the State Street station at 5:50am. With train Engineer Tom Dugan at the controls the on time passenger train picked up speed as it headed out of the city with a final destination of Buffalo. On board with Dugan were old time rail employees Conductor Charles A. Martin, Fireman Byron Nellis, Trainman C.J. Persons and Baggage-man Robert J. Frew. The passenger train with a locomotive, a tender, a baggage car, two passenger cars and a caboose had originated out of New York City, with several passengers on board and had made several stops along its route up the Hudson River to Albany. It was then onto Schenectady, Utica, Rome and Syracuse. With all these stops along its way to Auburn only two passengers, Lois Bennett and Elmer Caldwell remained on board. However, with several more stops along its western journey at depots in Aurelius, Cayuga, Seneca Falls, Geneva and Rochester many others would board and disembark.

Meanwhile at the Aurelius station a large NY Central freight train had been sitting on a side rail waiting for the passenger train to pass. The freight train due in Auburn at 1:55am, was several hours behind schedule due to terrible rain storms along its way. The freight consisted of a locomotive, a tender, thirteen freight cars and a caboose. Along with Engineer Emmett Lancott at the controls were Fireman J.G. Curry, Brakeman F.J. Ludolph and Conductor George Eighme. At approximately 5:40am, for unknown reasons, Engineer Lancott ordered the switch open and his train onto the main line. The move caused utter consternation among several of the railroad men present. But before anyone could stop the train, Lancott opened the throttle and the train moved quickly out of the station.

No one could have guessed what was about to happen next. As the two trains now on the same track picked up speed everything appeared alright. Within minutes of leaving their perspective stations both trains were at their top speeds, estimated to be around 25 mph. As they neared James Mullen's home in Aurelius, near Crane Brook in an area known as Flat Bottoms or Wheeler's Bridge, a short distance south of Auburn, they would encounter a steep down grade and pick up a little extra speed. They would also encounter a sharp curve making their forward view difficult, even more so due to the heavy fog and drizzling rain.

Only ten minutes out of their stations the two trains quickly closed in one another. As they rounded the sharp curve at Flat Bottom, Engineer Dugan on the passenger train suddenly saw the freight train headed straight at him. He quickly pulled the air brakes but it was too little, too late. The two trains met head on in what was described at the time as one of the most horrific train collisions in New York State.

Both engines smashed into one another with such force they became locked together and although neither had jumped the track they were stove in until their smokestacks touched one another. The tender of the passenger train was driven half its length into the engine and the cars behind it had all telescoped forward into one another. The tender on the freight train had been driven back against the adjoining freight cars and stood up on its end. The two locomotives were demolished and most of the freight cars had been reduced to kindling wood. Passenger train Conductor Charles Martin, injured by flying debris, had been in the baggage car with Baggage-man F.J. Frew. He managed to climb out of the destroyed car and hurried from the scene to call for aid. A mile down the track, at the H.C. Hemingway Canning factory, he managed to place a phone call to the NY Central depot in Auburn. Dispatchers there quickly notified City Hospital and the authorities. Coroner William R. Laird was also sent to the scene.

As rescuers began arriving they found Freight Engineer Lancott and Fireman J.G. Curry were pinned in the locomotive and had been crushed to death Their bodies had been crushed and scalded so badly they were almost unrecognizable. It took three hours and heavy equipment to remove their bodies. Baggage-man Frew had also been seriously injured. He was rushed to City Hospital but died three hours later. As they dug through the wreckage the body of an unknown man was found on the front platform of the baggage car. He had been crushed between the baggage car and the tender of the passenger train. At the time he was believed to be a tramp stealing a ride. Coroner Laird ordered his body be taken to Gross & Mosher Funeral Pallor at 3 Lincoln Street for a later autopsy. Engineer Dugan was thrown through his cabin window by the force of the collision and thrown several hundred feet away. He was in serious condition. Dugan's Fireman Byron Nellis, who had also been in the cabin, managed to jump from the engine just before the collision and escaped uninjured. Others injured were freight Brakeman L.J. Ludolph, Trainman C.J. Persons as well as passenger Lois Bennett, of 24 Barber Street, Auburn.

Scenes of the collision between New York central passenger & freight trains

It was reported that Miss Bennett, a teacher at the Aurelius district school, had been thrown through a window and suffered a deep cut to her cheek, injuries to both knees and a broken nose. She had somehow waded through the creek and up onto the roadway. With the assistance of passenger Elmer Caldwell she was able to walk to her home on Barber Street. She is now confined to bed suffering from severe shock. Reports indicate that she had returned home last evening and had caught the 5:50am train in order to get to the school on time, this being the only passenger train that stops at the Aurelius depot. Caldwell, the only other passenger on board at the time escaped without injuries. Freight Conductor George Eighme somehow had left the scene.

Within an hour news of the wreck had circulated throughout the city and a large crowd estimated to be close to 200 people had gathered at the scene. The fog and drizzle didn't deter the crowd as many stood by under umbrellas to witness the action. Several of the young people that had gathered were busy collecting the onions and grapes that had spilled from the freight train.

Later that afternoon, the body of the unknown tramp was identified as James E. King, of Skaneateles. Mr. King, age 26, was unmarried and was employed as a spicing foreman at the Seneca Falls Woolen Mill. He was formerly employed at Auburn Woolen Mill and Melrose Woolen Mill in Auburn. John O'Neil, proprietor of the O'Neil Hotel (later known as The Monroe Hotel), reported he had seen King jump the train as it passed the Monroe Street crossing in Auburn. It is believed King was en-route to his job in Seneca Falls. King leaves behind his parents, two brothers, Michael, an Engineer on the Skaneateles railroad, and George, of Harrisburg, Pa., and one sister, Mrs. Patrick McGinn, of Skaneateles.

In Auburn, NY Central station agent Michael Graney stated the blame for the accident laid entirely on the freight crew. He said it was standard operating procedure that passenger trains always had the right of way and that the freight train should have remained on the siding until the passenger train had passed. Coroner Laird stated that an inquest would be held to determine who was responsible. When asked if criminal charges would be brought he stated it was too early to say.

The collision closed one of the few connecting east-west rail lines and several freight trains were delayed while several more passenger trains were re-routed. NY Central wrecking crews and equipment were sent to the scene to remove the wrecked locomotives and rail cars. They worked late into the evening before the wreckage was removed and the track cleared for use.

Coroner Laird began his inquest the following day on Wednesday September 27th. All of the surviving train men were called to testify, along with Auburn station agent Michael Graney and night train dispatcher John B. Hamilton, plus James Mullin and James Morgan, both of Aurelius and the first persons to arrive at the scene of the wreck, passengers Lois Bennett and Elmer Caldwell, and several of the doctors that had treated the injured and or had performed autopsies of the deceased.

Of note during said testimony was Freight train Conductor Eighme's testimony that he had been asleep when his train left the siding, that he did not know when it left, and that he hadn't received orders or given orders for his train to move onto the main track. He noted that it was the first rest he'd had since 8:00am Monday morning. Much ado was made over the notifications sent station to station regarding the leaving and arriving of the trains via the railroads wire service. Dispatcher Hamilton stated that the wire service was working poorly that night and he had not received any reports that the freight train had left the Aurelius depot. On Tuesday October 10th, 1899, after the last witness testified Coroner Laird issued his findings. He stated none of the living trainmen, of either train is to be blamed and he exonerated the railroad company. He went on to say that the freight train was at fault for the accident, noting that its engineer Emmett Lancott had no orders from Conductor Eighme or special orders from dispatch to start his train onto the main line and further that he acted against procedures that require passenger trains always have the right of way.

As some interesting side notes: It was reported Conductor Eighme, resigned shortly after the accident. He had been a conductor for ten years. Passenger train Engineer Tom Dugan, of Canandaigua, the most severely injured person in the wreck eventually recovered. He had been a railroad man since his youth going on the road as a fireman, then a freight engineer and finally a passenger engineer. After time spent in the hospital and a month confined to his home he began making short runs again. However, the wreck wore on his mind and he suffered from melancholy. He never was the buoyant and genial spirit that made him so popular with the railroad men. On a run through Geneva he was compelled to look upon a fatal accident and his mind weakened. He was taken to Willard State Hospital. Confined there for two years he died there on Monday November 12, 1906. He was 50 years old. He leaves behind his wife, one son, three daughters and two brothers. NY Central attorneys settled Miss Bennett's suit for injures for $1,000.00.

Harvey C. Hemingway

While researching one subject I usually come across other interesting tidbits that would make a good story or at least an interesting story. H.C. Hemingway intrigued me so I had to do a little more looking around. Although he has nothing to do with the train collision, his factory in Aurelius was nearby and Conductor Martin called for assistance from there.

Harvey C. Hemingway was born on Wednesday January 22, 1851, in New Haven, Conn. He was educated in public and private schools of that town and as a young man entered into his father's business H.F. Hemingway & Co., a successful chain of wholesale and retail fish, oyster and fruit houses located in various cities from New York to Cincinnati.

While working at his father's offices in Rochester he married and with other associates from his father's firm he opened H.C. Hemingway & Co., a cannery in Brockport, NY. This plant was later moved to Clyde, NY. The company with offices in Syracuse grew and had plants in Clyde, Lyons and Aurelius.

In the canning industry, Hemingway was one of the best known men engaged in the development of machinery and methods in the early days of the business. He was an active supporter of its interests by service in both state and national associations.

Mr. Hemingway succeeded his father as president of H.F. Hemingway & Co. He was a life member of the Monroe Commandery, Number 12, in Rochester, and served as president of the Lockport Canning Co.. While living in Syracuse, he was a director of the Syracuse Trust Co., a member of the Citizen's Club and an active member of the Plymouth Congregational Church. He later moved to Auburn and resided at 49 Aurelius Avenue.

On Thursday January 29, 1914, a fire destroyed a storehouse owned by H.C Hemingway, in the town of Aurelius. The building was over 100 feet long and two stories high. The Auburn Fire Department sent Hose Co. 1, with Captain Fred Washburn in charge to assist. The men had great difficulty in getting the fire wagon through the muddy field to reach the fire. Although Crane Brook was nearby they were unable to draw a sufficient stream of water to apply to the fire. The estimated loss was $1,000.00 and $250.00 in farm machinery.

Mr. Hemingway died at his home on Aurelius Ave., at the age of 77, on Saturday June 30, 1928. He was predeceased by his wife Minnie in 1888, and is survived by two sons Roy, of Auburn and Stuart, of Syracuse, 11 grandchildren and two brothers. He was buried in New Haven Conn.

EDWIN L. THORNTON, THORNGREEN AND MERCY HOSPITAL

Edwin L. Thornton was born on March 30, 1837, in Fleming. He attended schools in Homer and Charlotteville, NY. Sometime later, as a young lad, he moved to Auburn with his parents William and Charlotte (nee Purchase), and resided on West Genesee Street. When 18 years of age he bought a large track of timber in the Fair Haven area and began operating a saw mill in that section. Lumber cut here was shipped to Oswego by boat. Between 1866 and 1877 he resided in Oswego and was extensively engaged in the lumber business with his uncle Seymour Thornton. He married Martha Knox, of Scipio and they had six children.

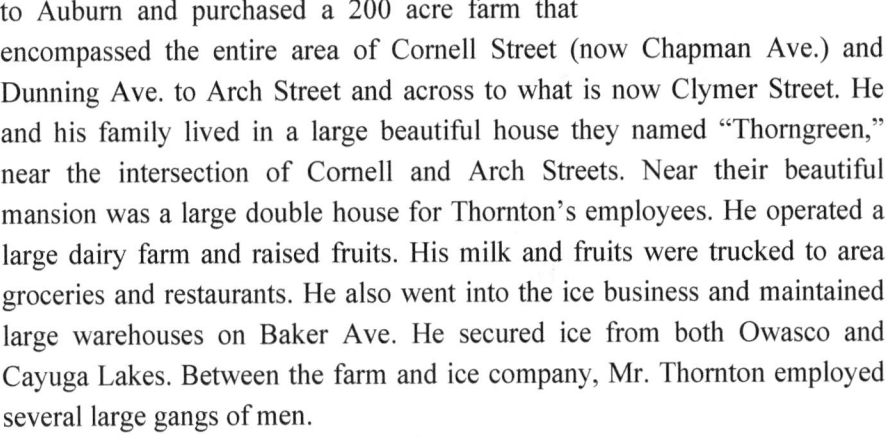

Retiring from the lumber business he returned to Auburn and purchased a 200 acre farm that encompassed the entire area of Cornell Street (now Chapman Ave.) and Dunning Ave. to Arch Street and across to what is now Clymer Street. He and his family lived in a large beautiful house they named "Thorngreen," near the intersection of Cornell and Arch Streets. Near their beautiful mansion was a large double house for Thornton's employees. He operated a large dairy farm and raised fruits. His milk and fruits were trucked to area groceries and restaurants. He also went into the ice business and maintained large warehouses on Baker Ave. He secured ice from both Owasco and Cayuga Lakes. Between the farm and ice company, Mr. Thornton employed several large gangs of men.

In his later years he involved himself in the real estate business, selling of tracks of his property for the development of new homes. He even financed the construction of thirty homes himself. Another 30 lots were sold to the Dunn & McCarthy Shoe Co. as they planned to construct affordable homes for their employees.

In 1903, Mr. Thornton sold his ice business to Wade, Shannon & Company of Penn Yan. In 1914, due to poor health, Mr. Thornton retired. He and his second wife Alzada (Martha died in 1890) moved to Ross Place. He sold what was left of the farm to local market men Cooper & Son. His home Thorngreen, the employees' home next to it and approximately three acres were sold to the Reverend William Payne, of St. Mary's Church. It was Rev. Paynes' desire, and that of the Rochester Catholic Diocese, that a Catholic hospital be built on the property.

Rev. Payne, in the twelve years since coming to St. Mary's Church, had been very successful in his endeavors. He had rescued the parish from bankruptcy, improved the school building and moved the Sisters of St. Joseph from their old and drafty dwelling on Hulbert St. into the former Barber estate at the corner of James and Clark Streets. Now he embarked on having a new hospital built.

Shortly after the Diocese took possession of Thorngreen contractors went to work converting the tenants' house into a twenty bed facility. Thornton's beautiful home Thorngreen was transformed into a nurses' home. In July 1917, Mercy Hospital was incorporated. The first Sisters of St. Francis arrived in September 1919 and the first patients were admitted in October 1919. In 1922 eight young girls made up the first graduating class of new nurses from the hospital's nursing school.

On November 3, 1930, amid a grand ceremony attended by several Church, City and County dignitaries and hundreds of local residents, the cornerstone of the new modern six-story Mercy Hospital was laid. A copper box coated with lead to preserve it was sealed and placed in the cornerstone. It contained a 1930 City Directory, copies of the Nov. 1st. issues of the Auburn-Journal and the Auburn Citizen, pictures of Rev. William Payne, who inspired and promoted the idea of the hospital and Rt. Rev. John Francis O'Hern, Bishop of Rochester, coins of the present day from a penny to a quarter, holy medals, a history of Mercy Hospital and the Hospital Guild along with their bylaws.

In 1972 the hospital opened the new seven story 297 bed Mercy Health and Rehab facility next to the hospital. In the mid 1970s the hospital started to fall on hard times due to rising costs, inadequate Medicaid reimbursements, the closing of the emergency room and operating suite and the reluctance of doctors to admit their patients. All attempts to keep the institution open failed and in 1977 the decision was made to close the hospital. In 1986, the old hospital building was renovated into apartments now known as Mercy Apartments.

Edwin Thornton was credited with developing the southwest corner of the city. He died in 1916 at the age of 79, survived by his wife Alzada, one daughter and one son. Thornton Ave. is named in his honor. Rev. Payne was also noted for his many contributions to St. Mary's and the City and especially his drive to make the Mercy Hospital project a reality. He died in 1925 at the age of 68, survived by a sister, a niece and nephew.

GEORGE F. WILLS

George F. Wills was born on Easter Sunday April 23, 1849, in New Liverpool, Quebec. His family moved to Auburn when he was a young boy. He attended Auburn schools and after graduating he obtained employment at the Packwood Carriage Co., in Skaneateles. He remained there until 1872, when he returned to Auburn and opened his own carriage shop on Clark Street.

In July 1887, he married Miss Jessie Bowes, of Auburn. They resided at 6 Elizabeth Street and had two children a boy and a girl. Mr. Wills was a well known and active city resident. He was a member of the Board of Education and a pass President of the Auburn Businessmen's Association. He served as an elected official and or committee member for several local civic groups including the Masons and I.O.O.F.. A lifelong member of the Republican party, he served on the Auburn Common Council as its President under Auburn Mayor Clarence Aiken. A number of times his party encouraged him to run for Mayor but he always declined.

His carriage and sled manufacturing company was very successful and was known throughout the northeast for their high quality craftsmanship. He continued in business until his retirement in October 1914.

Around 9:00pm Friday evening April 21, 1916, Mr. Wills was struck by a car while walking home and crossing the street near South and Elizabeth Streets. Two residents of 74 South Street, James Knapp and Paul Clark carried Wills into their home, called for an ambulance and summoned

Doctors Louis O'Neil and J.P. Craveling. Rushed to City Hospital all efforts to save Mr. Wills were futile and he died at 2:00am Saturday morning at the hospital. An investigation of the accident and inquest into the death was conducted by Police, Assistant DA E.J. Willis, Coroner Forman and Coroner's Physician Doctor William Walsh. The Police investigation determined that poor visibility at the time of the accident due to heavy rain and a street light not working were contributing factors. They report no vehicle or traffic violations occurred and no arrests were to be made. The Coroner reported death was due to injuries suffered, namely contusions from a scalp wound, fractures of both legs and membranous contusions and abrasions.

Ironically, Mr. Wills was buried on Easter Sunday April 23, 1916, in Fort Hill Cemetery, 67 years to the day of his birth Also of note, Mr. Frank Shaw Jr., of 19 Garrow St., the driver of the car that struck Mr. Wills had just sold the car earlier that day (of the accident) to Frederick Vandenburg, of 21 Burt Ave.. Mr. Vandenburg was so excited by his new purchase and anxious to take the car out for a ride that Mr. Shaw offered to chauffeur the Vandenburg family "outing." At the time of the accident they were headed back to Vandenburg's home on Burt Ave., just a short distance from where all their lives changed.

As an interesting side note... On Sunday November 10, 2013, the Citizen's "Look Back At The Lakes" column happened to look back ten years to November 10, 2003, when they happily looked into Throop resident Harold Short's garage where he shared his Wills made carriage and sleigh with his wife's sedan.

They report the carriage is a drop front Phaeton and belonged to his great-grandfather. The other a handsome classic black and maroon winter sleigh with ornate trim-exactly the type of transportation that would have inspired the Christmas tune "Jingle Bells."

It was reported the carriages are a way for Short to reclaim some of his family's heritage and the thing he loved most as a child. Short, who was 72 years old at the time of the article, still hitches his horse to the carriages several times a week to take a ride back through time.

Short's daughter reports "the carriages are the source of pride for my father. They're a connection with the family's history, something our family has preserved."

a drop front Phaeton carriage

GEORGE WILLS WAGONS

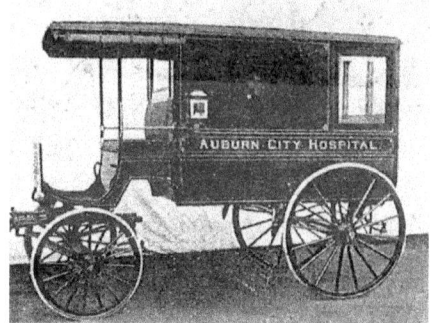

The above three wagons were manufactured by George Wills at his Clark Street shop. The newspaper's picture of the 1876 Auburn Police Department's patrol wagon noted that it could also be used at fire and accident scenes to save people's lives.

ALBERT H. HAMILTON: FORENSIC EXPERT OR CHARLATAN

In 2007, Auburn Police Sgt. Joseph DiVietro and I began researching old Auburn murder cases for a book we were writing. In 2008, we published our book *"Auburn Murder Stories"*. During the research, I kept coming across the name of Albert H. Hamilton. Mr. Hamilton made a living, through the late 1800s to the mid 1900s, as a criminologist. At the time he was considered one of America's first criminologists and his name appeared quite often as he was called upon by either the prosecution or defense as an "expert witness." I was a Detective and Evidence Technician and this interested me, but it wasn't until much later that I decided to do some research on Mr. Hamilton. What I found was quite  interesting. By some, Mr. Hamilton's scientific analysis of a crime scene, dead body, suspicious handwriting, blood evidence, firearms and gunshot wounds couldn't be doubted while others considered him a charlatan.

Albert was born in Weedsport on December 10, 1859, the son of James Theodore and Clarian (nee Hine) Hamilton. He attended Weedsport Union School and prepared to enter the US Naval Academy after graduation. For whatever reasons he declined his appoint to the Naval Academy, and came to Auburn where he apprenticed for four years as a druggist under Joseph N. Steel at Steel's Drug Store, on Genesee Street. He also worked as an accountant for a local grocery store during this time before deciding to enter the New York City College of Pharmacy. After his graduation in 1885, he returned to Auburn and worked for Steel as a pharmacist although druggist seems to be the more popular term used for the times. Sometime after he bought Steel's Drug Store and renamed it Hamilton's Drug Store. It was located at 51 Genesee Street. Here, Hamilton not only sold the usual prescribed antibiotics and medications but also his own mixed remedies to cure everything from baldness to indigestion. In 1888, he married Jessie Eccles and they had two children, a daughter Ruth and a son Robert. He successfully ran the drug store for twenty-five years.

1889 Newspaper ad

THE HAMILTON DRUG STORES,

51 Genesee St., (Branch, 80 Owasco St.) Auburn.

Wholesale and Retail Dealer in and Manufacturer of

High Grade Drugs, Chemicals, Proprietary Medicines, Sundries, Etc.

The proprietor of these stores positively refuses to recommend or endorse by newspaper advertisement or otherwise, any proprietary or patent medicine not endorsed by the reputable medical profession.

ALBERT H. HAMILTON, Proprietor.

His work as a pharmacist lead him to taking more of an interest in the field of chemical and microscopic investigation. He seemed to recognize that there was a shortage of criminologist in the justice system and in 1908 he published a brochure entitled "The Man From Auburn," in which he self promoted himself as a criminologist specializing in chemistry and microscopy analysis, hand-writing, fingerprints, guns and gunshot wounds, bullet and gun power identification, blood and other stains, causes of death, embalming and anatomy. It was reported he sent these brochures to every attorney in the state offering his services.

Shortly after publishing his brochure Hamilton became quite a busy man as District Attorneys' offices and defense attorneys from all over New York

State began calling on him to testify. Locally he assisted the Auburn Police, the Cayuga County Sheriff and District Attorney's office. Word of Hamilton's expertise spread and soon he was traveling throughout the States to offer his opinion on forgeries, murders, guns and gun wounds. He was able to charge as much as $50.00 to $100.00 a day for his services at a time when most people weren't making that much in a month

Although most of Hamilton's scientific analysis and testimonies usually went well it wasn't until he involved himself in several high profile cases that people and the courts began to doubt that what he was testifying to was actually fact.

Things began to unravel for Hamilton early on the cold snowy morning of Sunday March 3, 1915, just a mile from West Shelby, NY. Here, Charles Stielow, age 37, a semi-illiterate tenant farmer from Germany, and his brother-in-law Nelson I. Green had been arrested for the double murder of their employer 90 year old Charles Phelps and Phelps' housekeeper Marjorie Wilcott.

Charles Stielow

At Stielow's trial, Hamilton was called to the stand by the prosecution after Private Investigator George Newton, of Buffalo, testified that he'd obtained a confession from Stielow. Hamilton testified that bullets he'd tested fired from Stielow's .22 caliber handgun matched the slugs recovered from the victims' bodies, based on the bullets markings (rifling). He used photographic enlargements to prove his point. When questioned by the defense as to why he could not see the marks Hamilton was referring to, Hamilton took the photographs, looked at them again and replied "Unfortunately, I've photographed the wrong side of the bullet the marks are on the other side of the slug. Sorry about that." Hamilton continued that these marks were caused by nine scratches in the gun's barrel. The defense attorney looked down the barrel, shook his head and asked what scratches. Hamilton then explained that because of the tight fit, the explosive gases had followed the bullet down the barrel and filled in the scratches. He assured the jury that the marks had been there.

Because of Newton's and Hamilton's testimony, Stielow was found guilty of Murder First Degree and sentenced to death at Sing Sing's electric chair. His brother-in-law decided not to chance a jury trial and pled guilty to Murder Second Degree to save his life. He received a life sentence.

Through the efforts of prominent attorney Grace Huniston and Sing Sing Warden Thomas Mott Osborne (from Auburn & anti-death), who believed in Stielow's innocence, Stielow was granted three stays of executions. One of these stays was granted just forty minutes before Stielow's appointment with the chair after two other men confessed to the murders. How-ever, when they recanted his execution was re-scheduled.

Finally NY Governor Charles Whitman appointed a committee to review the case. The findings of the committee found Stielow's alleged confession suspicious and Hamilton's ballistic evidence flawed. They proved that Stielow's .22 hadn't been fired in years and test firings conclusively proved it wasn't the murder weapon. Stielow and Green were both released in May 1918. Neither received compensation for their time behind bars.

Saco and Vanzetti

In June 1921, Hamilton participated in the trial of Nicola Sacco and Bartolomeo Vanzetti. The two Italian immigrants were suspected anarchist militants who had been arrested for the $15,000.00 robbery and murder of a shoe factory paymaster and guard in South Braintree, Ma., on April 15, 1920. Testifying for the defense, he testified that after examining and test firing both of the defendants' handguns, they were not the weapons used to commit the robbery and murders. Part of his testimony was a demonstration in which he compared Sacco's handgun with two similar guns he'd brought with him to show the differences in the guns barrels and firing pins. In front of the Judge and jury he disassembled and reassembled all three guns, noting all the differences in the guns lines and grooves and firing pins. As Sacco's gun was returned to evidence, Hamilton prepared to leave the stand with his two guns in pocket only to be stopped by Judge Thayer. The Judge demanded that Hamilton's two handguns now be placed in evidence as they had been used as such during the trial.

The two defendants were eventually found guilty and sentenced to death. During the appeal process the defendants' handguns as well as the two Hamilton had submitted were examined and test fired again. During these closer examinations it was discovered that the old rusted barrel of Sacco's gun had been replaced with a new one from one of Hamilton's guns and Sacco's barrel was now on one of Hamilton's new guns. It was obvious that Hamilton had made the switch during his testimony and demonstration right in front of the Judge, jury, prosecution and defense attorneys. Hamilton admitted he had switched the barrels but stated he was mystified as to how it'd happened. His actions caused a furor and could have resulted in the release of the two defendants. Although he was never disciplined for his actions he was promptly dismissed from the defense team but not before submitting his bill for $2,800.00. Sacco and Vanzetti were again found guilty. Both were executed on August 23, 1927.

Shortly after the March 1932 kidnapping of Charles Lindbergh's baby son, Hamilton took it upon himself to examine the Lindbergh baby ransom notes. He went to Auburn Prison where he was able to compare hand-writing samples of incarcerated Albany gangster Manning Strewl to the Lindbergh ransom notes. After doing so, he declared Strewl had written the Lindbergh ransom notes. However, renowned document expert Albert S. Osborn disagreed with Hamilton's findings and the New Jersey authorities agreed with Osborn.

In August 1932, he was in Miami to testify for the defense of famous British flyer William Lancaster. Lancaster had been charged with the murder of American writer Haden Clarke. The motive....Lancaster's then girlfriend Jessie "Chubbie" Keith-Miller and Clarke were having an affair while the two corroborated on her autobiography. Despite over whelming evidence of Lancaster's guilt (aforesaid motive, the murder occurred in Lancaster's home, the murder weapon belonged to him and Lancaster admitted he'd forged the two suicide notes found at the scene) Hamilton testified Clarke had committed suicide. His testimony went better than the prosecution's experts and was well received by the jury. Lancaster was acquitted. Many believe Hamilton's testimony set a killer free.

In 1934, Hamilton found himself in Albany testifying for the defense of Albany gangster Manning Strewl. Strewl was being tried for the July 30, 1933 kidnapping of Albany Democratic powerhouse Dan O'Connell's 23 year old nephew John O'Connell Jr.. The young lad was held for 23 days before a negotiated ransom of $40,500.00 was paid for his release. Hamilton testified that Strewl hadn't written the ransom notes while other prosecution experts, particularly Albert S. Osborn, testified that he had. This put Hamilton up against Osborn again and under heavy cross examination he embarrassingly lost. Strewl was eventually found guilty and served 25 years behind bars. He died at the age of 95 at his home in Albany. The ransom money was never recovered.

By this time most prosecutors and defense attorneys were growing leery of Hamilton's testimony and he was pretty much forced into retirement. He reportedly had worked some 4,000 civil and criminal cases including 300 murders. He died at home, 162 E. Genesee St., on Friday July 1, 1938, at the age 79. He is buried in Soule Cemetery.

Was Hamilton a forensic expect or a charlatan? Many believe Hamilton to be a genius whose testimony resolved the guilt or innocence of their clients while others considered a self promoted fraud whose work was so flawed that it and his testimony should have never been allowed into a Court House. Many interesting books have been written about some of the aforesaid cases which go into a lot more depth on the subject matter and Hamilton's work and testimony.

As an interesting side note....The historic Steel Building, located at 59-61 Genesee Street burns. At 1040pm, Monday February 22, 1892, as Officer Ryan walked his North Street post and passed the alley way which leads to the back of the Steel Building he noticed smoke. Upon further checking on its source he saw flames rising from the second floor windows of Dundon's.

The Officer ran to headquarters, which was in the old City Hall building on North Street, and sounded the alarm. Dense smoke filled the air as the fire ate through the upper three floors fueled by druggist Hamilton's drugs and extracts and fly paper making materials of oil and bees wax. Although the building's cut stone façade looked to be sturdy and fireproof it was basically a wooden structure and no more than a tinder box after the fire took hold.

Firefighter John Titus was overcome by smoke and Firefighter Gus Emerick, on the upper rungs of a ladder and holding a hose, lost his balance and nearly fell. A cheer from the large crowd, estimated to have been up to a thousand onlookers, meant he successfully held on. Firefighters fought the stubborn blaze for five hours before bringing it under control.

The losses were considered substantial. Druggist Albert Hamilton took the biggest lost. He estimates his losses at $11,000.00, insured for $7,000.00; Mill & Lathrop Gloves & Mittens, no estimate of damage, insured for $1,500.00; Lightfoot & Pike barbershop, value of property $3,000.00, insured for $2,000.00; E.C. Stanley's Teas, no estimate of damage, insured for $2,000.00; Dundon's Variety Store, estimated loss $3,000.00, insured for $2,100.00. The building itself was considered a total loss. It had been built by Eleazer Hills in 1822.

William Dundon and his wife operated Auburn's first Five and Ten Cent Store.

BREWING IN THE PRISON CITY

In the mid 1800s through the mid 1900s, Auburn boasted at least seven breweries and several more bottling operations. Some of these old breweries were producing 5,000 to 20,000 barrels of brew yearly, most of which was drank in the city and neighboring towns. Brewing families like Koenig and Burtis made small fortunes.

Here is a list of some of Auburn's better known breweries:

1) Burtis & Co., located at 34 Water Street, began in 1849. One of the City's largest originally began as Burtis & Cornell. Later operated as Burtis & Son.

2) Sutcliffe Brewery, located at 88-90 Clark Street. With eight employees, they produced 5,000 barrels of beer and ale a year.

William Koenig

3) Independent Brewing Co., located at 117-127 Clark Street. At the height of their success they employed forty-six men and had six wagons to keep up with the demand for one of the area's most popular brews.

Independent Brewing, 117-127 Clark Street

The above building, before becoming Independent Brewing had once been home to Sutcliffe Brewery, Ehrman Brewing Co., and The American Brewing Company. When the Prohibition Amendment went into effect in 1920 it pretty much closed all these city breweries. Shortly after closing, this plant began a new life as a milk plant. In later years the building was torn down and a new building was built for the Dairymen's League. The League building was torn down to make way for the City's new arterial highway.

4) The Fanning Brewery, located at 6-10 Garden Street. Employed fourteen men and produced 5,000 barrels a year. Later became NYS Brewing, later used for storage for Manroe Brewing Co. until bought out by Bartels Brewing of Syracuse.

The Fanning Brewery, later NYS Brewing, 6-10 Garden Street

5) C.A. Koenig & Co. Brewing, located at 6-14 Grant Street. Their specialties were Bohemian Lager and Cream Ale. They also produced a full line of sodas. The men that built this company also owned a popular summer hotel and dance pavilion on Owasco Lake and provided transportation there via their steamers City of Auburn and Nymph.

Koenig & Co. Brewing, 6-14 Grant Street

6) Cold Springs Brewery, located 132 York Street. Amazingly, they were able to use the spring water located on their site to produce their products.

Cold Springs Brewery, 132 York Street

7) Holmes Bottling Works was located at 39 Garden Street, at the rear of the NY Central RR Depot. Holmes started bottling lager beer but eventually branched out into bottling mineral water, ginger ale and other soft drinks. His products were very popular and enabled him to hire five men and use three wagons to make deliveries in the City and outlaying towns. In 1912, the business was being operated by Wall and Haverin at 29 Water Street.

Early 1900s C.A. Koenig ads

Koenig ads often referred to their product's purity and good health qualities. Note that they were "highly recommended by physicians" and "imparts vigor to the languid and the convalescent."

As some interesting side notes....On Thursday morning June 2, 1898, Ehrman office employees were quite startled when they opened for business and found the company safe had been "cracked open" and $190.00 missing.

It was reported two suspects, an ex-con named Brando from Geneva and a tramp named Mitchell had been taken in by Police but later released. Brando was turned over to Geneva Police on Burglary and Larceny charges in that city and Mitchell was "driven out of town." The paper reported foot patrol Officer Arthur Titus was on duty when the burglary occurred. They stated because of his large walking beat, from Hulbert Street west to the city line (a distance of one mile) and from Wall Street to Orchard Street (a distance of ½ mile), the crooks were assured they wouldn't be interrupted. The paper stated the Police believe the crooks were no spring chickens as the burglary was very similar to those committed in neighboring Port Byron, Moravia, and Wayne County. The paper noted that Auburn needed at least 20 more officers to ensure affordable protection for its citizens and their interests or else the crooks would surely be heard from again.

In August 1900, after several Auburn brewers signed criminal complaints, John W. Burtless, a junk dealer on Water Street, and Soloman Kaletzka were arrested for dealing in stolen bottles. Bail for the men was set at $500.00 each. It was reported Kaletzka planned on shipping the stolen bottles to Syracuse. 465 of the stolen bottles were recovered in the NY Central warehouse. Brewers retrieving the stolen bottles were Ehrman—58, Holmes—130, Koenig—133 and Walter Conway—144.

FARM EQUIPMENT AND WAGONS

For more than 50 years, from the mid 1800s through the mid 1900s the manufacturing of farm reapers, mowers and wagons dominated Auburn industry and contributed to its prosperity and growth In 1865 there were six establishments located in Auburn manufacturing mower-reapers and other farm machinery.

The largest of these companies was the D.M. Osborne plant located at the corner of Genesee and Mechanic (Osborne) Streets. The complex ran from the aforesaid corner south up Mechanic St. to Lincoln St. and encompassed the entire area where Wegmans is located today. The company had offices in Philadelphia, Chicago, St. Louis, Kansas City, Dallas and San Francisco. They shipped their products all across the US and to Canada, Mexico, South America  and Europe. Railroad tracks were laid out from the NY Central railhead on State Street that ran along the south side of the outlet, crossed North Street then emerged through a tunnel, to cross Genesee Street and run up Mechanic Street to service the plant. In 1904, a special train of forty-two cars loaded with Osborne harvesters left the factory bound for Russia. At one time 4,000 men were employed here. International Harvester eventually bought the Osborne plant and continued operations until 1950.

R. THOMAS BURGER

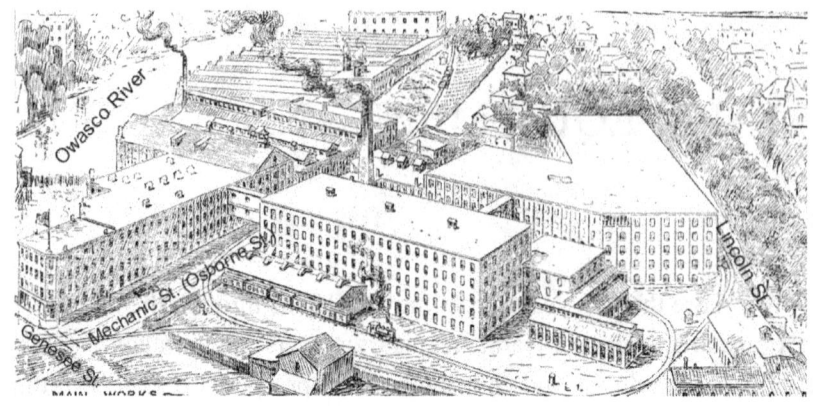

Other large manufacturers were Hussey & Co., located on Mechanic Street (Osborne St.), later bought out by D.M. Osborne. Dodge, Stevenson & Co., originally located in Genoa they moved to Auburn after their plant burnt down. Located on Washington Street, they used the Owasco River to generate power. Cyrenus Wheeler's "Cayuga Chief" was originally was manufactured in Popular Ridge. They then moved to Aurora to facilitate shipping by train and boat. Their machines were also manufactured at Auburn Prison before a large plant was built at the end of McMaster Street. This building also became the home of Burtis & Beardsley until both companies were bought out by D.M. Osborne. In July 1865, many of these reapers and mowers were put to the test at Stewards Corners, in Venice. In an exhibit they were put through their paces in a field of wheat owned by Benjamin Fordyce. Osborne, Dodge & Stevenson, Hussey, Burtis & Beardsley and the "Cayuga Chief" all had machines present.

This was an era when horses were the main source of transportation and labor in the field as most of these machines were horse drawn. Therefore, several other companies were manufacturing wagons and wagon parts. Two of the largest manufacturers were E.D. Clapp, located at the corner of Genesee and S. Division Streets (Columbus St.), and The Eagle Wagon Works, located at 43-47 Columbus Street. The Eagle dump wagon became one of their specialties. When the automobile started to take over the roadways these companies diversified and began manufacturing auto parts.

As a note of interest....the building at the end of McMaster Street, in later years, became the home of The Wegman Piano Co. and later Auburn Plastics. It still stands today, occupied by Volunteers of America and The Auburn Trading Post.

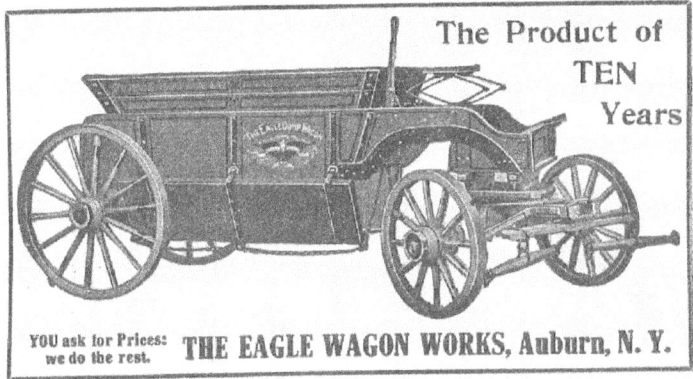

The Eagle Wagon Works' motto:
"Quality, rather than price; How good, rather than how cheap."

Their printed literature often contained the phrase
"If you need a dump wagon and don't buy an Eagle, we both lose money."

RAIL CITY

Throughout the 1800s and into the early 1930s one could catch a horse drawn or an electric powered trolley to make their way around the city. The trolley company Auburn Inter Urban Electric R.R. became the Auburn City R.R. until it merged to become the Auburn & Syracuse Electric Railroad. Their tracks, usually located in the center of the street, ran from the east end to the west end and from north to south You could catch a trolley to get to Owasco Lake and the parks or to Syracuse. Because of its central location, Auburn was also on the main line for just about every train, whether freight or passenger, headed to just about anywhere in the state that had a depot. Rail lines such as the Southern Central, Auburn & Lansing, Lehigh Valley and the great New York Central all ran through Auburn at one time or another.

Today the only rail service operating in Auburn is the Finger Lakes Railroad, headquartered in Geneva. The company began in 1995 running on the tracks once used by the NYC ("the Auburn Road"), Lehigh Valley and the Pennsylvania Railroads. They operate mostly locate freight but three or four times a year the rail company offers scenic passenger rides known as "Heritage Tours."

As a kid, I can still remember seeing some of those trains that pasted through town and occasionally the old trolley tracks poking through sections of worn roadway. The following pages offer a glimpse into some of the great Auburn depots, trains and trolleys that ran through the city.

NYC RR Depot, State St.

Lehigh Valley Freight

Freight Crossing Columbus St.

Southern Central RR

Trolley on Genesee St. at South St.

Auburn Trolley

Trolley barn, Franklin St., area of East Middle School

GENERAL CLINTON D. MACDOUGALL

Clinton Dugald MacDougall was born near Glasgow, Scotland on June 14, 1839. In 1842 his parents immigrated to Canada and then moved again to settle in Auburn. He graduated from Jordan Academy in 1852 and went on to study law. However, in 1856 he gave up his legal studies to become head bookkeeper at the Auburn Exchange Bank. In 1860 he partnered with William H. Seward Jr. to establish the Wm. H. Seward & Co. Bank located at the corner of Genesee and Exchange Streets.

In April 1861, after South Carolinians fired on Fort Sumter, MacDougall was instrumental in raising the 75th NY Volunteer Infantry. Mustered in Auburn, he was appointed Captain at the age of 22. That winter the regiment left Auburn and was transported to the Florida area. In May 1862, while on a nighttime scouting mission near Pensacola, MacDougall was wounded when Union pickets mistook him for the enemy.

Returning to Auburn to recuperate, he almost immediately began recruiting for another new regiment. In August 1862, MacDougall was appointed Lt. Colonel of the new 111th NY Volunteer Infantry. The regiment left Auburn and was transported to Harpers Ferry, W. Virginia. The under trained and ill equipped men were present when Confederate General Thomas "Stonewall" Jackson attacked Harpers Ferry in September 1862. Under constant attack for three days, Jackson was handed a victory when Union Colonel Dixon Miles surrendered the post and its 12,000 defenders.

The men spent approximately a month as prisoners before being pardoned and exchanged for prisoners. The regiment continued to serve in every battle with the 2nd Army Corps including Gettysburg, The Wilderness, Spotsylvania and Appomattox. At Gettysburg the unit was center stage during Pickett's charge and MacDougall was wounded again. During the course of the war, MacDougall was wounded four times and had six horses shot out from under him. He was promoted several times reaching the rank of Brevet Brigadier General.

When the war ended he declined a position in the Regular Army and returned to Auburn. In 1867 he married Eva Sabine. They had three children a son William and twin daughters Margaret and Jessie. Eva died shortly after giving birth to the twins.

MacDougall was appointed Auburn Postmaster in 1869 and was elected to Congress in 1873, a position he held until 1877. During this period of time he was offered the positions of US General Counsel of either London or Paris, Secretary of the Treasury and Director of the IRS. Each time he declined. He did accept the position of US Marshall for the Northern District of NY in 1877, a position he held until 1909.

In 1878 he married a second time to Marianna Cook. In 1886 he and Marianna moved from 30 South Street to their newly built mansion at 108 South Street. The elegant house was a showplace. The beautiful and expansive Italian garden contained a fountain and the grounds were tended to by a head grounds man and two gardeners. The MacDougall's large dining room was the scene of many formal balls and the grounds were the scene of many Union soldiers' reunion picnics. The MacDougalls also bought the adjoining Boyd estate for the use of Marianna's cousin Mary Chedell Beardsley.

The MacDougall estate had large servant quarters and a carriage house built behind it that in later years were converted to apartments on present day MacDougall Street (the street was named in his honor). Next to these buildings they built tennis courts. They also owned property on Burt Ave. that was used as servant's quarters. The household staff consisted of a household manager, three maids, a chauffeur, a cook, a waitress and the garden staff.

MacDougall continued to be active in Auburn's civic and business life. He was influential in establishing the Soldier's Home in Bath, NY and the Gettysburg Battlefield Memorial. He was also President of the New Birdsall Co., Vice-President of the Board of Trustees at the Soldier's Home, a member of the Grand Army of the Republic, the City Club and the Owasco Country Club. In his later years, as his health began to fail, he would spend winters in Paris at the estate of his sister-in-law. It was here, on May 24, 1914, that he died. After funeral services in Auburn, he was buried in Arlington National Cemetery with full military honors. Marianna continued to reside at the South Street mansion until her death in 1925. The home and property was then bought by Theodore Case. Mr. Case eventually removed the mansion and Boyd estate to build his own mansion---the present day Case mansion. At the time, Case's mansion's was the largest home in Auburn.

The MacDougalls' home and gardens were so beautiful that postcards of the estate were made and sold locally. On a Sunday drive many people would pass by to admire the home and gardens.

WEST SIDE MURDERS AND HAUNTINGS

Benjamin Harris was born in Auburn on Sunday January 19, 1800. He was the second child of James and Sally (nee Wright), and his sister Sarah was nine years old when he was born. The family lived in a nice house on Grover Street. His father was a successful grocer with a well stocked store on North Street. As a young boy Ben would help his father around the store. When he was old enough he would hitch their horse to their wagon and make deliveries. They were one of the few stores around at that time to make delivers. Many believed that helped make them so successful.

Ben was a well liked and smart boy who attended Auburn schools and graduated at age 17 near the top of his class in 1817. By this time both his mother and sister had died. Although his father wanted him to run the store, Ben yearned to see New York City. Within three months of graduation he boarded a train at the State Street depot and was on his way. Once in the city, Ben found a job in a grocery store and a small apartment not too far from the store. His new neighbor was a young lad named John Brigsby, a 19 year old southern boy from a wealthy family. The two hit it off and did everything together. In May 1834, John finally decided he'd had enough of the "big city life" and invited Ben to accompany him home to South Carolina. Ben agreed to go. They were met at the train station in Donaldsonville, SC, by a handsome carriage driven by a well dressed Negro man who loaded their belongings and took them to Evergreen, John's family estate. It was a large plantation, some 1,200 acres of cotton and tobacco. The house was a large red brick mansion with four tall white columns supporting the roof over a large white railed front porch where the family would take their refreshments in the afternoon. John often bragged that his father was wealthy, making his money on the cotton and tobacco trade and that "the old man" owned 155 slaves that lived about a quarter of a mile down the road from the main house. The family had Negro slaves working as cooks, servants, gardeners, coachmen and in the fields. John's father had a black personal butler and his mother a black chambermaid.

After a month of what seemed like a vacation Ben took his savings and moved into Donaldsonville. The town was about four miles from Evergreen and had a population of 8,700. It was a busy hub of business activity being that it was centrally located between Savannah and Charleston and on the main line of the Southern Freight and Passenger Rail Service. Ben loved his new found home and the laid back style of the south With the little money he had left and help from the Brigsbys he opened a successful grocery store that in time allowed him to buy a saloon and rooming house. He became a very successful and wealthy Southern gentleman.

Ben Harris

In June 1845, a small plantation became available when its owner died leaving no one to inherit his 500 acre estate. Ben sold his store, saloon and rooming house to buy the property. At the age of 45, he became a plantation owner raising cotton with 23 slaves and a couple of hired hands to oversee things. He named his new home Auburndale.

One of Ben's hired hands, a six foot three, muscular 240 pound hard drinking 40 year old named Wesley Bunn, was a man that had served time for murder. He seemed to have no feelings for the suffering slaves he oversaw. Wes was known to freely use the whip and one time he beat a male slave so badly the man almost died. The other hired man, a 35 year old named Harold Crumby, called Hank by his friends, wasn't much better. The two men drove the slaves, with few breaks, from daybreak until sundown. Ben didn't seem to care. His take on all of it was that's just the ways things are….the work needed to be done. He had even been known to take a whip to the back of a lingerer. He had truly taken on a southern way of thinking.

In January of 1858, Ben received news that his father was in ill health Ben traveled to Auburn and stayed for two weeks. In his absence, his good friend John Brigsby over saw operations of Ben's plantation. When he returned to Auburndale he told John he was selling the place and moving back to Auburn. This was at a time when wealthy plantation owners were living large and it didn't take long for one of them to buy up Ben's property including 11 of his 23 slaves. It seems during Ben's two week stay in Auburn, he had bought a 200 acre farm near the western boarder of the city. His plan was to bring Wes, Hank and his remaining twelve slaves to the new farm where they would grow wheat and corn. Now in 1858 slavery didn't exist in New York State let alone in Auburn, the home of Harriet Tubman and William H. Seward. These facts didn't seem to faze Ben who had by now grown accustom to the Southern way of life.

In March of that year Ben had secured four covered wagons to transport his belongings, Wes, Hank and his twelve slaves to Auburn. After crossing the Mason-Dixon Line, and not wanting to get caught transporting slaves north, they kept to the back roads to avoid nosy people and prying eyes. Two and a half weeks later they rode into Ben's new farm. The house wasn't as large as Auburndale but was sufficient enough for his needs. Approximately 400 feet behind the house were three out buildings to be used as living quarters for Wes, Hank and the twelve slaves. Beyond that there was a large barn and just off to the side of it a smaller one for equipment. Ben named his new home Maple Grove.

Now Ben's instructions to Wes and Hank were to work the slaves while keeping them out of sight….no one was to know they were there. Of course the two men took these instructions to mean they could do anything necessary to make the slaves work and never be seen or heard. The eight male slaves were made to construct an eight foot wooden stockade around the two outer buildings used for the slave quarters. That spring when Baraka, a 32 year old slave, refused to leave his bed Wes beat the man so badly that he died from the injuries. Wes made sure that no one would ever know, he had Baraka's body taken to a large fire pit and burnt beyond recognition. The remains were then buried deep in the woods.

Also that spring Ben's father passed away. Ben took over the store but hired young man to manage it. With a successful store and crop planted Ben lived quite well. He was well known around town and highly admired. He was a member of several local organizations and associated with most of Auburn's prominent families. But that was soon to change in 1863 as the American Civil War continued to tear the North and South apart.

In April of 1863, as the war raged on, Ben's slaves learned that President Lincoln had promised all slaves their freedom via the Emancipation Proclamation and they began a little rebellion of their own. They refused some work, took breaks when they needed to and stood up to Wes and Hank. Now Wes' temperament wouldn't allow for "these niggers to do whatever they want to do." On Wednesday May 13th, Wes had reached his boiling point when a young 18 year old boy refused to work. When Wes went at him with his whip the boy grabbed a pitchfork and put it right through Wes' stomach. When Hank went to assist his buddy he was met with an axe to his head. It was an instant death As Wes lying bleeding to death he was put out of his misery by the axe wheeler who placed a well aimed chop to the back of his head. Now in a frenzy the slaves set fire to Wes' and Hank's living quarters. Upon hearing the commotion Ben grabbed a six shooter and ran outside to see what was happening. It proved to be a fatal mistake as four of the slaves jumped him and beat him to death After setting Ben's home on fire they gathered up what belongings and necessities they could, hitched two wagons and headed out.

John Gardener of Half Acre happened to be passing by as the slaves drove away from the property and he could clearly see that there was a large fire burning behind Harris' home. As he pulled his carriage up to the main house he yelled for Ben. Receiving no answer he quickly walked around to the backyard, where he saw the two outer buildings and the rear of Ben's home ablaze and the dead men lying on the ground. Running back to his carriage he quickly made his way to the Sheriff's Office on Court Street to inform them of what he'd seen. The Auburn Fire Department along with the

Auburn Police and Sheriff's Deputies rushed to the scene. The three dead men were all known to the arriving rescuers. An alert was immediately dispatched to all nearby Police and Sheriff's Departments to be on the lookout for 7 Negro males accompanied by 2 or 3 Negro females traveling in two white canvas covered wagons.

At eleven o'clock that night the group believed responsible for the murders and fire were found near Ithaca where they'd set up camp for the night. They were held until the Sheriff made arrangements to bring them back to Auburn.

Within two days the slaves were brought back to Auburn and placed in holding cells at the jail. Under intense questioning the leader of the group, a 35 year old named Sam confessed to killing all three of the men and setting the fires. The sheriff's men were appalled to learn how these 11 black slaves had been transported from South Carolina to Cayuga County and kept as slaves on Harris' farm. The investigation uncovered their terrible treatment and poor living conditions and the many hours of toil and abuse they had endured. After learning of the murder of Baraka, a search was made of the area where his remains were buried. Lead to the spot by Sam the only thing ever recovered were four teeth set in a jaw bone.

The Sheriff's continuing investigation brought out the fact that Harris had been supporting the Confederacy with the use of his home as a safe house for Confederate messengers and spies running between the southern states and Canada. And that he'd sent funds to the confederacy via his good friend Confederate Colonel John Brigsby. When the local newspapers broke the story the people of Auburn and surrounding towns were appalled and shocked. Many who knew Harris couldn't believe he owned slaves, that the murder of a slave had occurred on his property or that he had supported the Confederacy. They had believed him to be a gentlemen and Union loyalist.

Perhaps feeling sorry for the slaves and having a confession in hand, the Sheriff didn't pursue any charges against any of the other slaves. The District

Attorney agreed and the remaining slaves were released. It is noted that during this time period slaves seldom had or ever used last names. When the need arose they would generally take or be given their masters' last names. This probably had more to do with who owned the slave and it worked well when Sam was brought to court to be arraigned on the murder and arson charges as Sam Harris.

A May Grand Jury upheld the murder and arson charges against Sam and a June trial date was set. The trial began on Monday June 8, 1863. Defended by Auburn attorney Alan Green the defense had little to work with except to play the sympathy card. The trial took two days and the jurors took only forty-five minutes to find Sam guilty of all three murders and arson. Perhaps some sympathy played into Sam's sentencing since the usual punishment for such a crime was hanging. Sam was sentenced to serve 40 years at Auburn Prison.

Many people in Auburn felt Sam should have been set free, that the murders were somewhat justified and his life since being brought to the states as a young boy and sold into slavery had never been free and now never would be. Ten years later, at the age of 45, Sam was finally set free when he died in his prison cell. He was buried in the unclaimed prisoners' lot at Fort Hill Cemetery. Many years later those prisoners buried here were re-interred in mass graves at Auburn's Soule's Cemetery, located on Franklin St. Rd., in Sennett.

After Sam's death an article appeared in the local paper rehashing the entire Harris story. It was accompanied by a short poem titled "Sam," written by an unknown poet. Here is a copy of the poem:

Sam
Once a boy roaming free
'til caught and bound
And taken to the land of liberty
Forced to work under the whip
'til he broke and his master he killed
Now in a five by seven cell he sits
'til the good Lord takes him in death
No freedom for Sam exists

No one ever bought the Harris property and it eventually became so run down the county ordered it to be torn down. But that wasn't going to be the end of the story. Twenty years after the murders a group of young boys decided camping along Crane Brook one night would be fun. The spot they picked was on what had previously been Harris' farm. Little did they know they wouldn't be getting too much sleep. As their camp fire burned and they drifted off to sleep, they were all awoken by what sounded like men arguing and screams and moans of what they later described as men fighting and dying. It was so eerie the boys left their gear and headed home. Over the years others passing by the Harris farm, particularly on early moon lit mornings, reported hearing men arguing and seeing a man wandering around as if lost. A local farmer named Joseph Abate reported on one occasion as he passed the old Harris property he saw a man wandering around the property that he thought might have needed help. Abate said when he stopped to offer assistance "the man just vanished." Many people believed the site of the Harris farm and murders to be haunted and avoided it all together.

As the years passed and the "old timers" died off the story of the slaves, murders and haunting faded into history and have long ago been forgotten. Today the old General Electric plant sits on the site where one of the county's most bizarre episodes, murders and perhaps hauntings occurred. Could the souls of Harris, Wes, Hank or Baraka still be present and searching for their eternal rest?

THE UNION ARMY FIGHTS IN AUBURN
75TH NY VOLUNTEER INFANTRY & THE INVALID CORPS

Often, while researching one subject I find myself seeing something else that strikes an interest and off I go on another project. And although I find researching a subject can be fun it can more than often be very frustrating.

So, there I was researching a subject when down in the corner I saw an article on the 75th NY Volunteer Infantry. Naturally I had to read it and what I found surprised and intrigued me so much that I knew I had to write about it. Finding information on the 75th NY Volunteer Infantry was somewhat easy. There are rosters of the men, lists of the officers and the battles they participated in. However, finding the information I wanted on the one particular incident I was looking for seemed impossible.

Searching across the internet (including Fulton History's website), consulting with Civil War buffs, a trip to Seymour Library's History Room, even email questions sent to the National Archives and the NYS Military Museum, I received several suggestions but kept coming up empty handed. I even consulted a professional Civil War researcher, but at $40.00 an hour and no guarantee she would find the paperwork I wanted it all seemed hopeless. Anyways, I found the story so intriguing that I'm going to write about it with the little bit of information I do have.

In 1860, as the differences and tensions between the North and South continued to escalate, particularly after the election of Abraham Lincoln to the Presidency of the United States, most people believed it would all be worked out and if came to a war it would be a short affair, maybe a month or two.

All of their hopes for no war or a short war were quickly dashed when several Southern states began seceding from the Union and on April 12,

1861, the first shots of war were fired at the Union flag and garrison at Fort Sumter, South Carolina by the newly formed Confederate Army. After those first shots both the Northern and Southern states began calling for large numbers of volunteers to join their armies. The American Civil War would rage on for four more years.

On July 21, 1861, after a Confederate victory at Bull Run, President Lincoln called for more volunteer troops. In response, NY Governor Edwin Morgan issued a proclamation calling for 25,000 NY volunteers. That September, Lt. Col. John A. Dodge, of the 49th NYS Militia met with several prominent citizens of Auburn and Cayuga County. His plan to raise a regiment in Auburn and to arm, equip and train the men here was well received. Recruiting began on September 7th, and was done principally in Auburn and Cayuga and Seneca Counties, although men enlisted from all over the State. By September 10th, Clinton D. McDougal reported with his minimum filled. He was quickly followed by two more companies on the 12th. Having been promoted to Colonel, John A. Dodge was named commander of the newly formed regiment now referred to as "The 2nd. Auburn Regiment." By October approximately 30 acres of suitable land in the Moravia Street (later re-named Lake Ave.) and Swift Street area was found for a camp dubbed "Camp Cayuga." Here the men were trained for their new life in the Army. The camp name was later changed to Camp Seward, in honor of Auburnian and Secretary of State William H. Seward. The regiment received their numerical designation on November 14, 1861, and was mustered into service on November 26, 1861 (nine companies) for three years. The regiment embarked for the south on December 6, 1861. Six days later they were stationed at Santa Rosa Island and Fort Pickens, Florida, for their first winter of service.

By 1862, as the war raged on, many of the soldiers became disabled, wounded or sick and could no longer serve on the front lines. At first these men received medical discharges but as more and more men were needed for the front lines the Army allowed those disabled men who could perform to take up non-combat duties such as cooks, nurses, or guards thus freeing up able-bodied men for combat duties. By 1863, the Army created the Invalid

Corps, two battalions of worthy disabled officers and men who were or had been in the Army. The first battalion was for men who could bear arms and perform guard duty at supply depots and prisoner camps. They also provided details to escort prisoners, recruits and assist the Provost Marshall arrest deserters. In 1863 they helped quell the "Draft Riots" in New York City. On March 18, 1864 they were re-named the Veteran Reserve Corps. In July of that year they manned the defenses of Washington, DC, during Confederate General Jubal Early's raid against Fort Stevens. The second battalion was for the men who were handicapped and fit only for mess, office or hospital duties. These two battalions were also organized into companies and regiments. Late in the war the Surgeon General took command of the second battalion.

 The 75th NY Volunteer Infantry went on to fight battles in Louisiana, Texas and Virginia. In October 1863, they were re-assigned to General Nathaniel Bank's Army of the Gulf as a mounted cavalry unit. Over the course of the war they participated in the siege and capture of Port Hudson, La., the battle at Sabine Pass, Tx., General Bank's Red River Campaign and General Philip Sheridan's Army of Shanandoah pursuit of General Early through the Shenandoah Valley in Virginia. At Port Hudson, La., and Sabine, Tx., they took heavy losses and many were captured.

 In October 1863, while still in Louisiana many of the veterans of the 75th, with their term of enlistment nearing an end, re-enlisted. In January 1864, these re-enlisted veterans returned to Auburn on a month furlough while the newer members were re-assigned to keep the 75th active in service. It was during their furlough that an incident occurred between these furloughed members of the 75th and a unit of the Invalid Corps assigned to guard Camp Seward. The Invalid Corps was also assigned to patrol the city streets while members of the 75th were in town, much like today's MPs would do. The men of the 75th were battle tested and despised the idea of being supervised by men they considered "stay at home soldiers." There were many fights and arguments and a lot of hard feelings between the two units.

Old Invalid Corps NYC recruiting poster

As the furloughed men reached Auburn they expected to be paid. When they weren't inquires were made to New York State officials. The answer from Albany was "since they had re-enlisted in Louisiana they were no longer considered a New York State regiment." Somehow the State now recognized them as a Louisiana regiment. This answer infuriated the men who questioned why anyone would consider them a regiment from a rebel state when everyone knew they were from New York. To top things off, in March they received orders to report to Washington, DC, for re-assignment as an infantry regiment. Not only hadn't they been paid, now their furlough had been cut short and they had been re-assigned from a cavalry regiment back to an infantry regiment. The men had been promised by General Banks that they would remain with him as a cavalry unit. Their grievances were sent to the Army but they were told nothing could be done about it. They requested to be kept on leave until their grievances were resolved and asked for Secretary of State William H. Seward's intervention. They even sent a petition to President Lincoln, all to no avail.

So on Saturday March 26, 1864, they were marched down Genesee Street to the train depot on State Street, escorted by members of the Invalid Corps. At the intersection of Genesee and North Streets words were exchanged between the two units and what the newspapers later described as "a mini-riot" broke out between the two units. Several members of the Invalid Corps fired upon the men of the 75th. Two members of the 75th, Elliott Ausitn, age 18, and Charles Roberts, age 24, were killed. Sergeant Clement was seriously wounded as was another private. Regimental records show that Austin had enlisted in Lansing on September 29, 1861, also that he had been wounded at Port Hudson, La.. His death was listed as "killed in riot, Auburn, NY." Roberts' record shows that he had enlisted in Marcellus on March 3, 1864, only 23 days before he would be killed on Union soil. His death was listed as "killed resisting provost guard, Auburn, NY."

The citizens of Auburn who happened to be on the street watching the men marching by were now running for cover. They couldn't believe what they were seeing and hearing. Had the Confederates and the war come to Auburn? As the sun rose Sunday morning and the news of the shooting spread, the citizens of Auburn, Cayuga and Seneca Counties were not only shocked but outraged. The 75th Volunteers were hometown boys, how could Union soldiers fire on other Union soldiers? Many blamed the state for not paying the men and not recognizing them as a New York regiment. Others blamed the Army for cutting their furlough short and re-assigning them back to an infantry regiment. Still others blamed it on the drunkenness of both units involved and the hard feelings between the two units. Many questions needed to be answered.

And this is where my problem started. I wanted to know more....who were the commanding officers of these units at the time of the incident, the number of men involved and more importantly was an investigation conducted and if so what did it say? Surely this would have been a big news story and covered by newspapers all over the Country. However, as I searched and searched I found no newspaper accounts of what happened after the incident. Most Civil War buffs didn't even know of the incident and researching on line resources provided no further mention of it. Even searching the on line National and State Military History sites I found nothing more regarding this incident. One reason I couldn't find anything locally I'll explain at the end of the story.

This much I do know....the men of the 75th got on the train and reported to Washington, DC. They heroically continued to fight in Louisiana and Virginia and participated in General Sheridan's victory at Cedar Creek, Va., which effectively ended any future Confederate invasion of the north In January 1865, they were assigned garrison duties in Savannah, Ga., where on August 31, 1865 they were mustered out. During its service the regiment lost

8 Officers and 122 enlisted men killed or mortally wounded; 2 officers and 67 enlisted men by disease or other causes, for a total of 199 men. Ten men died in the hands of the enemy.

Between 1863 and 1866, some 60,000 men served in the Veteran Reserve Corps performing vital non-combat duties for the Union Army. The Corps was abolished in the summer of 1866.

As an interesting side note.....while researching this incident I found one local newspaper article in which an unidentified member of the 75th wrote to the local newspaper on April 27, 1864, from a camp near Washington, DC.. This is a copy of the newspaper's article and the letter:

The 75th Regiment.
We regret to find that there is still a strong feeling of dissatisfaction prevailing in the 75th Veteran Volunteers. It appears that the regiment re-enlisted under the promise, made by Gen. Banks, that it should serve in the future as Cavalry, and this promise the War Department has been unwilling or unable to perform. We were confident at the time of the outbreak at Auburn, that that discreditable affair was not merely the result of a drunken row, but originated in a deeper feeling. We have received the following from one who professes to be a member of the regiment, but as he does not give his name, we should not know what credit to attach to it, were we not aware from other sources that there has been an unfortunate mistake with regard to this regiment. It has gained a very honorable reputation for its courage, and the fidelity with which it has performed its duties, a reputation which, we trust, it will maintain, even if the members feel that they have just cause for complaint. It has to be remembered that the Government cannot, under the changing circumstances of the war, always perform what the soldier has a just right to ask and expect:
CAMP OF THE 75TH N. Y. VET. VOLS.
NEAR WASHINGTON, AP. 27, '64.
MR. EDITOR:—If there is any one who respects honor it is the soldier—he who has left his home and friends and all who are near and dear to him to fight for the glorious Union. And, Mr. Editor, in so doing that soldier expects the Government of the United States will see him justified in all his rights, and has he not a reason to expect this? I think so. But we, a regiment of men who have served the United States' Government honestly and faithfully for two years and a half, and have re-enlisted for three years more as Veterans, claim that we have not had these privileges shown us and feel it deeply.
We re-enlisted at New Orleans as Cavalry, went home on a furlough of thirty days, and, when that had expired, were ordered to report at these head quarters. Here the authorities at the War Department do not recognize [sic] us as Cavalry, inasmuch as we enlisted under a special order of Gen. Banks.
The War Department has issued orders that no soldier shall be enlisted under false pretenses. I would like to know what they can make of this but false pretenses. Had we known that we would have had to serve as infantry, there would not have been money enough in the State of New York to have persuaded us to re-enlist. Had they ordered us to New Orleans, we would have had that branch of the service for which we enlisted.
I do not think that the Government of the United States can say but what we have always done our duty like men, when in the hour of danger, and will always continue to do so. We were given the post of honor at the surrender of Port Hudson, by an order of Gen. Banks, for our services rendered there, and is this the way the government is going to reward us for our services? I hope not.
There was a committee appointed to call upon Hon. William H. Seward, Secretary of State, inasmuch as the regiment was from his native State, and from his own city Auburn, thinking that perhaps he would use his influence in our behalf, but the reply was that he would do nothing for us, and, moreover, that the officers of the Regiment had said enough about the matter already to dismiss them from the service.
Now, Mr. Editor, I have no doubt, in my mind, that had we been a Regiment of the darker colored men, but he would have used his influence in our behalf. I honestly think he would. We, however, as soldiers from the county of Cayuga and city of Auburn, thank the Hon.
    William H. Seward for what he has done for us.
    Will you be kind enough to publish this in your paper, and oblige an enlisted man of the 75th N. Y. Vet. Vols.

Colonel Dodge, while serving in Florida became very ill. In July 1862, he submitted his resignation and was honorable discharged on July 22, 1862.

Now for the rest of the story....While at Seymour Library's history room I learned something interesting. Back in the late 60s or early 70s, when the Citizen was moving from their old Dill Street building to their new facilities across the street, they asked the library if they would be interested in their old newspaper collection which dated back to the early 1800s. Of course the library wanted the collection. Over the years the library made the collection available for us to view on micro-film. They also made these newspapers available to Fulton History and that's how we get so much information from that site. Now the thing is, when I went there to research the 75th and Invalid Corps incident I was informed that the newspapers for that time period weren't available. It seems back when the transfer of the Citizen newspaper collection to the library was taking place the Civil War era newspapers, 1861 thru 1865 went missing. No one seems to know if they were misplaced, destroyed or stolen?

I often wondered why I could never find photos from that time period or of the Civil War units from Auburn. And, where were the newspaper photos of Secretary Seward, General Grant, Colonel Custer and Captain Myles Keogh who all visited Auburn during this time period? To this day no one knows what happened to these newspapers....a huge important era of our history is now missing forever.

Nothing remains of Camp Seward. However, if you are driving along Lake Avenue near the Camp Street intersection there is a historical marker noting that the Civil War Depot was located in this area.

A NILES MURDER MYSTERY

William Dennis, age 38, lived with his wife Maria and their four children, ages 3 to 17, out in the town Niles, near New Hope. He was the town constable and well known. On Wednesday May 10, 1871, he had been gone most of the day running errands and had been to Dutch Hollow on official business. It was close to sundown and a frost was settling in, as he headed home and his horse became ill. He stopped at neighbor Jacob Lewis' home to rest the animal. After spending some time at Lewis', the horse appeared better and Dennis decided he'd better get back on the road. It was 1100pm, and Lewis thought he should spend the night and make towards home in the morning, but Dennis was anxious to get home and set off.

Upon reaching home and getting the horse to the barn, he found his wife had turned in. However, his entry awoke her and she inquired as to what had kept him. After explaining his stop at Lewis' due to the sick horse, she asked if he would bring some tomato plants in, afraid they'd be injured by the frost. It was midnight as he finally made his way to the bedroom and prepared for bed. As he stood in his bedroom undressing a shot rang out, its projectile broke through the bedroom window instantly striking Dennis in the head, he fell to the floor dead. His wife and family immediately ran to his aid but it was too late. His son Willie rode to neighbors' homes for help, the first one being the home of Henry Day Sayles.

Henry Day Sayles was 38 years old and somewhat of a handyman. He worked various jobs, had at one time been employed by the Dennis family and was currently working for John Carpenter who operated a mill and distillery at the upper falls on Appletree Point Road (Carpneter Falls is named after his family). Sayles was also known for his hard drinking especially when he became intoxicated and threaten either his family or anyone else who happened to be present and fall under his dislike at the moment.

It was just after sundown, on Wednesday May 10th., when Sayles had finished working for John and Dwight Dennis and headed home. He was exhausted and upon reaching home he found his wife visiting with neighbor Maria Ryan. After sharing pleasantries, he went to bed. His slumber would soon be disrupted and his life changed forever by the shouts of a terrified Willie Dennis "someone shot pa. Please come help."

Henry quickly got up and dressed and ran to neighbor Abram Jones' home. On his arrival he found the Joneses had also been awaken by Willie Dennis. Minerva Jones was dressed but said she was too scared to go out and asked Sayles to take her daughter Hattie to his house. After he complied, he returned and he and Abram made their way to the Dennis' home. When they arrived they found some others neighbors were already there and the Dennis family grieving. J. Bishop Partello, who seemed to be in charge, asked John to stay and help out until the Sheriff Deputies arrived. By 300am, Deputies Orisimus Van Etten and Thompson Keeler arrived along with Coroner and Doctor William Cooper. The investigation began.

An autopsy revealed Dennis had been killed when a bullet entered his skull behind his right ear, passed through his brain and exited approximately two inches above his left eye. His skull was severely shattered. It was reported that many of the lead slugs had lodged in the wall and ceiling, one as large as the end of a man's finger. A Coroner's inquest determined Dennis had been murdered by an unknown person. By July 1871, a Grand Jury convened by DA William B. Mills, had heard enough evidence to indict Henry Day Sayles for the murder of Dennis. He was arrested shortly thereafter, arraigned and sent to County Jail charged with Murder First Degree. If Sayles was found guilty he would face the death sentence.

The announcement of the arrest shocked many people but not all. Several had said Sayles had held a grudge against Dennis and on several occasions had threatened to either cause him bodily harm or kill him. The DA knew it was going to be a tuff case to prosecute as most of the evidence against Sayles was circumstantial.

The trial began on Monday October 14th, 1872. Judge Darwin Smith would oversee the trial. DA Mills, assisted by E.G. Lapham, of Canandaigua, would prosecute and David Mitchell, of Syracuse, assisted by James Lyons, of Auburn would represent Sayles. In his opening statement DA Mills stated that Sayles believed Dennis had had criminal sexual intercourse with his (Sayles) married daughter Caroline (Sincerbox) and even with his wife Eliza. That he would show because of these beliefs along with the problems his daughter Caroline's marital separation created and Dennis' probing of the distillery that it was Sayles and Sayles alone that murdered Dennis.

The list of witnesses, most from Niles and New Hope, was long. Most of them knew both the Dennis family and Sayles family. The list included Mrs. Maria Ryan, Edwin Dodge, William Helmer, Jirah Cady, Warren Williams, William Slade, William Wood, Matilda Baker, Charles Johnson, Abram and Minerva Jones, Peter Rynders, William Pidge, Jailor Elijah Field, Sheriff Deputies Van Etten and Keeler, Doctors Lansing Briggs, of Auburn and William Cooper, of Kelloggsville and Dennis family members his brothers John and Dwight, his wife Maria and son William (Willie), age 18, and Sayles' wife Eliza Jane and their 15 year old daughter Emma. Henry Sayles also took the stand in his defense.

Doctors Lansing Briggs and William Cooper, testified as to being called to the Dennis home after the murder, their examination of Dennis' body and the murder scene and their autopsy and findings. Both agreed Dennis had been shot in the head by a high powered weapon, such as a shotgun. They described his wound and how they'd located at least 5 pieces of lead (buck shot) on and in the head wound. They stated other pieces of lead were found in the bedroom ceiling and wall.

Willie Dennis testified that, after the shooting, as he rode up to Sayles' home he thought he saw a shadow in the doorway, that the door was open and someone was entering the house. He said, however, when he finally got to the door it was closed and no one was there. Further, that he yelled at least three or four times before John Sayles finally came to the window and asked "is your pa shot?"

From the very beginning there was controversy over foot tracks many of the witnesses had seen in the frost at the window where the shot had been fired and horse and buggy tracks not far from the window that crossed a nearby field. It was the opinion of many of the witnesses that these foot tracks lead to Sayles' home and that the imprint seemed to match Sayles' boot. Deputy Van Etten had even measured Sayles' boots. Other witnesses swore they hadn't seen any foot prints crossing the field toward Sayles' home and those that were found later that morning were made by the many people crossing to and from Dennis' home after the murder. Some witnesses also testified to hearing a horse and buggy headed to Dennis' before the murder and after the murder hearing it speeding away. There were some who saw the tracks of the horse and buggy and others that didn't.

Controversy also erupted over alleged threats made by Sayles against Dennis. Some said they'd heard these threats while others said they had been made when Sayles was intoxicated and had been taken out of context. Most of these alleged threats concerned Sayles belief that William Dennis was ruining his family life in that he'd (Dennis) had had a sexual relationship with Caroline Sincerbox (Sayles' daughter), and with his wife Eliza.

Still many others believed that Sayles had committed the murder on behalf of his employer John Carpenter. It was said that Dennis, as the town Constable, had been causing trouble for Carpenter's distillery. The distillery had made Carpenter a wealthy man and kept Sayles employed. Neither man would have wanted it shut down. Since a recently fired shotgun was found in Charles Ryan's barn the day after the murder, many believed Sayles placed it there while fleeing the scene of the crime. Testimony was given as to whether Sayles had a gun or had access to Carpenter's or Ryan's guns. More issues were raised when John Jones testified that bullet moulds, a half pound of No. 3 or 4 shot and four or five charges he'd kept at Sayles were no longer there.

When the prosecution ended its case the defense immediately asked that the charge be dismissed in that the prosecution hadn't proven their case beyond a reasonable doubt. That their evidence was all circumstantial and heresy and they hadn't offered any evidence that directly connected Sayles with the murder. The Judge overruled their request.

When Sayles took the stand he denied he killed Dennis. He stated although he may have made threats against Dennis, he did so when intoxicated but otherwise he had no hard feelings for the man. He denied he had access to a gun or had used either Carpenter's or Ryan's guns. He stated he had sold Jones' bullet moulds and other items. He told the Court and jurors that Dennis had been to his home many times and that he had been to Dennis' home many times. He admitted that he had used a pocket knife in an attempt to commit suicide after Dennis' death and that his son-in-law Charles Sincerbox prevented him from doing so. Sayles testified that upon arriving home on the night of the murder, he found Maria Ryan visiting with his wife, further that after exchanging pleasantries he went to bed and never arose until Willie Dennis woke him. He said he heard Willie yell once and never asked him if his father had been shot. It is noted that his bedroom was located off of the kitchen where his daughter Emma was sleeping and she had testified that she had been sleeping in the kitchen, had seen her father enter his bedroom for bed and never saw or heard him leave until Willie woke everyone.

On Tuesday October 22, 1872, the defense rested. At 2:00pm, Mr. Mitchell made his final arguments to the jury, taking two hours to do so. After a dinner break, Mr. Lapham took approximately an hour and a half to present the prosecution's final argument. By 1000pm the jury retired to deliberate. At 1030pm, the jury announced they had their verdict and pronounced Sayles "Not guilty." The Court room erupted with applause and Sayles offered the jurists "my sincere thanks." He was discharged and quickly left the Courthouse.

Many persons believed Sayles was guilty or had acted on the orders of John Carpenter. Others believed it was a member of Carpenter's family that committed the murder. In the end, who actually killed Dennis will never be known. No one was ever arrested or tried for the murder after Sayles was found innocent.

As some interesting side notes....John Carpenter was a well known and wealthy resident of Niles. He ran a mill and distillery at what is known as Carpenter's Falls (named after his family) on present day Appletree Point Road. The building, a rather large structure, was located next to the bridge and between the road and the edge of the falls. Much of the "brew" produced here was transported down to Skaneateles Lake where it was loaded onto boats and taken to Skaneateles to be sold. Sources say it operated between 1825 and 1870 or '75, when the government imposed heavy taxes on spirituous beverages. Naturally, ways of avoiding these taxes came about. So when "a revenue man" was on his way to check on activity at the distillery, Carpenter side tracked him long enough for his trusted employee Henry Sayles to open a trap door allowing several barrels of "brew" to roll down into the gorge and out of view of the revenuer.

Sometime after his acquittal Henry Day Sayles and family moved to Auburn. He ran a boarding house and saloon on Garden Street, near the NY Central RR depot. He eventually moved to Moravia and ran a butcher shop. Still prone to drink, he was intoxicated and ornery on Saturday evening September 6, 1879, when he told his little grandson that he was going to kill himself. The boy informed his father but the threat wasn't taken seriously as Sayles had often threatened to kill himself while under the influence. However, this time it would be different. Between 900pm and 1000pm, he was found dead---he had hung himself in his barn behind his home and business. Coroner Cox was immediately called to the scene but determined an inquest would not be necessary. He ruled Sayles death a suicide.

Diagrams of murder scenes as shown in the newspaper.

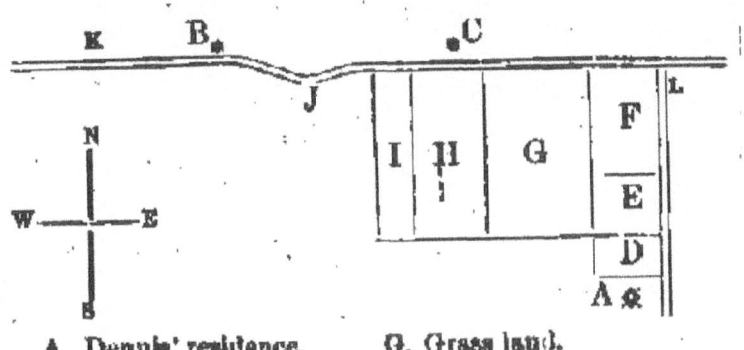

A. Dennis' residence.
B. Bayles' residence.
C. Abram Jones' residence.
D. Plowed field.
E. Growing wheat.
F. Grass land.
G. Grass land.
H. Jones' meadow.
I. Plowed strip.
J. Gulch.
K. New Hope & Skaneateles [Lake Road].
L. Lane.

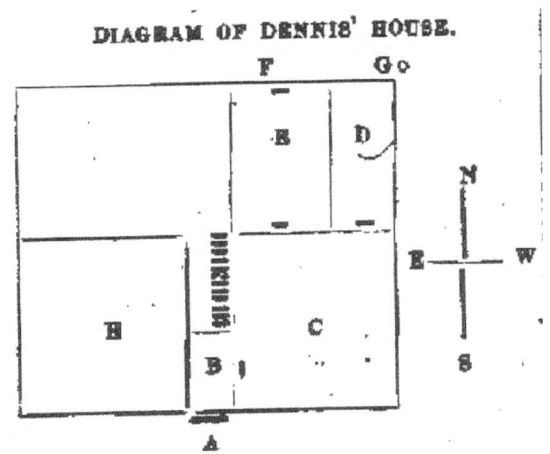

A. Outer door.
B. Hall.
C. Kitchen.
D. Pantry.
E. Bedroom where Dennis was shot.
F. Windows.
G. Tub of water.

A MURDER IN WEEDSPORT

In 1873, Edward Flynn, was 49 years old and had been running a saloon in the downtown area of Weedsport, for ten years. He and his wife Margaret lived in the small apartment above the saloon with their 20 year old daughter Maria. Flynn had been born in Ireland and immigrated to the US in 1846. He wore a "spring leg," as his left leg had been amputated from the calf down after an accident in 1852. His saloon has been called a vile and disreputable groggery. As such, he was known as "one of the worst men in the village," and his wife was known to be quite quarrelsome when drunk.

The day before Thanksgiving, Wednesday November 26, 1873, was not going to be just another day for Flynn and his wife. Around noon Flynn opened his saloon and noticed a stool was missing. When his wife arrived a short time later he asked her about it and the two began arguing. By then a few men had arrived to quench their thirst. When they paid for their drinks, Mrs. Flynn demanded her husband give her the money. He complied as the men paid for another round and she again demanded the money. Only this time she was angry….she paced the room with a poker and called him very harsh names. He gave her the money and she left.

Mrs. Flynn returned to the saloon sometime later that afternoon and was very upset. She told Flynn that she and Maria had been arguing and that Maria had taken the money. She told Flynn that he needed to lick Maria. He told her that since she was older than Maria she could punish her as well as he could and she left. Later Flynn learned that his wife and daughter had quarreled again and that it had gotten physical, the two of them slapping each other and pulling one another's hair.

Between 800pm and 900pm, Flynn went upstairs and told his daughter Maria that he was going to bed and that she ought to do the same. At approximately 1000pm, Flynn was awoken when he heard Maria yell "papa, papa, I am stabbed with a knife." He sat up on his bed and while trying to put his pants and boots on he yelled to Maria "who is it?" Then he heard someone in the hallway. He yelled "who's there," and then saw a figure in the darken bedroom doorway. The figure swung something at him, he raised his hand to block the object and felt a sharp pain. Realizing that he had been stabbed, he struck the figure twice with his boot before he heard the unknown person fall to the floor. By this time Maria came into the room with a lantern. When Flynn saw who lay on the floor he exclaimed "Maria, it is your mother!" Margaret laid on the floor bleeding from a wound to her head. While Maria stayed with her mother Flynn ran out to get help. He found Charles Coyle and a few other men and returned to the house with them. They put Margaret in bed while someone went to get a doctor. A short time later Doctor Fordyce Benedict arrived and dressed the woman's wounds.

Mrs. Flynn was confined to either her bed or the couch recovering and all seemed fine until Saturday the 28th.. That evening, between 1000pm and 1100pm, she took a turn for the worst and by 1100pm she died. Early Sunday morning Coroner William Foster traveled to Weedsport to conduct an inquest into Mrs. Flynn's death. The inquest which concluded on Monday afternoon found that she had died from at least three violent blows to her head by an unknown object causing several fractures which resulted in an inflammation and compression of the brain causing her death. The coroner ruled the death a homicide. By Monday evening Edward Flynn and his daughter Maria had been arrested for the murder and were in the custody of the Sheriff.

The January Grand Jury indicted Flynn for the murder of his wife. His daughter escaped any further legal problems when they returned with a no bill. Flynn pled not guilty at his arraignment and District Attorney William Payne moved for a trial date of Tuesday January 20, 1874. Auburn attorneys Patrick Deering and William Mills will represent the defendant. Judge Charles Dwight will preside.

The first witness called by the prosecution was Doctor Benedict. His testimony related to the night he was called to Flynn's and attended to Mrs. Flynn. He stated on his arrival he found Mrs. Flynn in bed, her hair was clotted with blood and her shoulders were covered by blood. He noted a wound on the left side of her head and two more serious wounds on the right lower back of her head behind the ear. One of these wounds was a ½ inch and the other one inch in length. He stated he was able to stick his finger in the larger wound and found the bone (skull) fractured. Doctor Benedict told the Court that Mrs. Flynn said something that was unintelligible and after attending to her and dressing the wounds he told her husband to keep her in bed. He said he returned the following morning and left after he found the premises locked and no one answered the door. The doctor continued....that he came back later Friday evening and found Mrs. Flynn on the couch. "I asked how her how she felt, she tried to answer but was unable to do so. Flynn and I placed her back in bed. I returned Saturday, she seemed to be gradually sinking, I left medicine for her and she died that evening." The doctor stated that he was present at the post mortem examination and related their findings and aforesaid cause of death. He told the Court that Mr. Flynn, who was present on Wednesday evening when he'd been called to treat Mrs. Flynn, had told him that he had been in bed, heard an unknown person in the hallway, that it was dark and he did not know who it, that he was struck by a knife and hit the unknown person with his boot. He stated that Flynn then showed him a wound on his hand allegedly caused by a knife.

Others called to the stand were Doctors Brown, Briggs and McCarty, witnesses Charles Coyle, Harvey Coppernoll, Mike Franey, John O'Connor, George Wamsgars, and a Mrs. Riley and Mrs. Coyle. The doctors' testimony confirmed Dr. Benedict's as related to the post mortem examination and cause of death. The others testified to what they'd seen and heard relating to the day and evening of the incident involving the actions of both Edward and Margaret Flynn and their daughter Maria. They all had been in the Flynn saloon and home during the day and after the incident. They'd seen Margaret bloodied on the floor. Interesting testimony related to the scuffling and hair pulling between Mrs. Flynn and Maria and Maria chasing her mother with a broom stick. Most felt Mrs. Flynn was in a foul mood and intoxicated when she demanded money from her husband and argued with Maria. O'Connor noted that he'd seen Mrs. Flynn with a poker when she demanded money from her husband and that she threatened "to kill him." Mrs. Riley and Mrs. Coyle both stated that while in the Flynn home, with Margaret lying on the floor, Edward remarked "let her die there (on the floor), I'll kill anyone who summons help."

The Court room was full the afternoon Maria was called to the stand. She stated that on the day her mother was injured she had snatched some money from her and the two of them scuffled....slapped each other and pulled one another's hair. She admitted she had chased her mother with a broom handle but "only in fun and I never struck her with it." She said she and her father went to bed between 8:30 and 9:00pm, at that time her mother was out in front of the house sitting in a wheel barrow. Maria said that she was awoken when someone stabbed her and she yelled to her father. She said it was dark, she lit a lantern and went to her father's bedroom, that he was in the hallway and said someone had stabbed his hand. That we went to the bedroom and mother was lying on the floor. I saw blood on her head and the floor and a crowbar next to the door. She continued....father told me he did not know it was mother, and not to let anyone in while he went to get help. She stated that she hadn't told anyone about her wound or shown it to anyone before being jailed. She also said that she hadn't been drinking and was not intoxicated.

On Wednesday January 21st., Edward Flynn also took the stand in his defense. He related his version of the day and evening of the incident as previously stated. He admitted that he'd been arrested twice for assault, once with a hammer. He also said he'd been arrested six times for selling liquor without a license. He stated most of what Maria had told the Court was false. He swore that in the darken bedroom he didn't know who stabbed him and thought someone was in the house that was out to kill him....that it was either "Mike or the Irish nigger" (a reference to his step-daughter that had married a Black man). He stated he struck the unknown person twice with his boot and denied he'd used a crowbar.

The case was given to the jury at 1:15pm. At 6:15pm they returned their verdict of guilty of Manslaughter 2nd. Degree. Edward Flynn was sentenced to serve six years six months at Auburn Prison.

As an interesting side note....On Friday July 31, 1880, only seven years after the death of her mother, 26 year old Maria died of consumption at the home of her father Edward, of 29 North Street, Auburn. Both father and daughter had "served their sentences."

OLIVER CURTIS PERRY
"THE LONE WOLF BANDIT"

While the Wild West had the James Gang, Billy the Kid, Butch Cassidy and The Sundance Kid, central NY had Oliver Curtis Perry. A descendent of Oliver H. Perry, the hero Commodore of Lake Erie, Oliver Curtis Perry was born on Saturday, September 17, 1865, in Johnsonville, near Troy, NY. While still a young boy his parents moved to Syracuse where his father Oliver H. Perry worked as a contractor. His mother died shortly after their move and his father, unable to work and care for the youngster, placed Oliver in an Oswego County orphanage. There is some evidence that he attended grade school at West Amboy, in Oswego County. Young Perry was a restless lad and at the age of eleven he ran away from the orphanage. By the age of twelve he had been sent to the Elmira Reformatory on a burglary charge. The Rochester Penitentiary soon followed. Upon his release he told his family and friends "Things are too hot for me in this State," so he hopped a freight train and traveled the country riding the rails. He settled out west where he obtained work as a cowboy. Working as a ranch hand he became quite efficient with six shooters and lassoing. But, he couldn't stay out of trouble and at the age of nineteen he stabbed and killed a fellow worker over a card game in Montana. Escaping the consequences he made it to Minnesota only to end up spending time in prison there for a robbery. He also did time in Wisconsin on another robbery charge.

Upon his release he hopped the freights again and made a living wherever he could find work. He returned to the Troy area where he met Amelia E. Haswell, thought to be the only woman he ever loved. At the time she was teaching a bible class and she encouraged Perry to attend. She had a calming effect on the young man and through an acquaintance she found him work as a brakeman for the NY Central Railroad. He may have had ambitions on marrying Amelia and buying a house but he soon realized by earning $2.00 a day he wasn't making enough money to save let alone survive and this is when he made a decision that would change his life forever.

OLIVER C. PERRY.

On Wednesday September 30, 1891, when the NY Central American Express Special, Number 31, pulled into the Albany depot to change engines, Oliver was there to meet it. The Express Special consisted of ten cars and was known to carry large sums of money and valuable property between New York City banks and banking houses further west. While the rail men went about their tasks Perry managed to slip into the vestibule of the express car. Here, hidden in the dark, he waited until the train pulled out of the depot to make his next move. While clinging to the outside of the fast moving train, and nearing Utica, he managed to cut a hole through the express car door. The hole, only 15" x 17", was just large enough for Perry to climb through. Once inside the car he announced himself to express messenger E.A. Moore by placing his revolver to the surprised messenger's head. "Don't move or do anything foolish," Perry said as he grabbed the messenger's handgun, carelessly left out where he couldn't retrieve it. With that he made Moore lay on the floor, and looking over his shoulder said "Keep him covered Jim, if the damn fool wiggles let him have it," as if speaking to an accomplice. He quickly moved about the car ransacking bags and packages that not only contained cash but jewelry all the while keeping Moore covered with his handgun. Once he had taken his bounty he backed out of the car onto the vestibule and cut the brake air hoses. That caused the train to immediately start to slow down. Upon reaching a slower speed Perry jumped from the train and disappeared into the night.

As soon as the train reached Utica an alert was sent out. An intense search of the area failed to turn up the robber. Authorities estimated his take was $5,000.00 cash and $3,000.00 worth of jewelry.

Ah....but this wasn't going to be the last anyone ever heard from the daring "Lone Wolf Bandit," as the local press began referring to the robber. So successful was his first robbery that Perry couldn't stop himself for pulling off another one.

On Sunday February 21,1892, Perry waited patiently on the loading platform at the Syracuse depot for the American Express Special to leave the station. Unbelievably, he was going to rob the same train again!

Perry boarded the train just as it began to pull away from the depot. He then hid himself on the platform between two cars and waited until the train had left the Syracuse city limits before making his next move. Nearing Weedsport he climbed to the express car's roof, secured a rope ladder fitted with a strong metal hook, to a cornice on one side of the roof and lowered himself down the other side to a window. This was all done while the train gained a speed of 50mph. His plan so far was going as well as he'd planned.

Daniel McInerney

Reaching the window he smashed it out with the butt of his handgun and calmly swung into the express compartment surprising messenger Daniel McInerney. Yelling at McInerney to "throw up your hands," McInerney answered with a shot from his handgun. Perry returned fire and wounded McInerney, striking his wrist and knocking the gun from his hand. Perry ordered the messenger to "stand still or be filled with lead," but McInerney reached for the signal cord only to be shot again. This time the bullet grazed his temple and he fell to the floor unconscious. Perry then went about his business of gathering up his booty. By this time other crew men grew suspicious of the noise coming from the express car and went to investigate. However, they quickly retreated when Perry fired several rounds at them. As the train passed Port Byron Perry exited the express car and climbed to the roof. Just outside of Lyons the train slowed for its scheduled stop, Perry jumped off and disappeared.

At the Lyons station the train men quickly learned what had happened to McInerney and a doctor was summoned. As that was being done Perry calmly walked into town from the other direction and stood on the station platform with the excited crowd that had gathered. But, the conductor recognized him as the man he'd seen at the Syracuse depot. Realizing that he hadn't seen Perry on the train since they'd left Syracuse, the conductor yelled "You're the man I saw in Syracuse, you're the man that shot the messenger." As the crowd turned on Perry he pulled his two revolvers and yelled "Oh no boys, don't be in such a hurry." With that he made a dash across the rail yard with the crowd in pursuit. Not far away was just what Perry needed, an unoccupied running locomotive sitting on open track. Being an old rail hand he uncoupled the freight cars, jumped aboard and put the steam to the engine. As he pulled out of the station the pursuing trainmen uncoupled their cars and started the Ole '31 after him.

As the two engines raced down the tracks, Perry realized the '31 was quickly catching up to him. He stopped his engine, threw it into reverse and as the two engines passed one another he fired several shots at his pursuers, only to be fired on himself with the only weapon the train men had time to obtain....a shotgun.

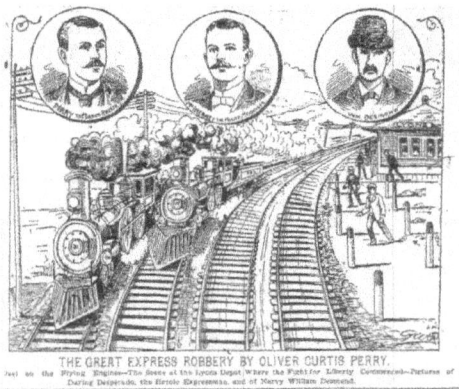

The train men threw their engine into reverse and took up the chase again. However, by the time they accomplished that Perry had reversed direction again. More shots were fired as the two engines passed one another again but no one was struck. Realizing they were out of ammunition the train men returned to Lyons and Perry continued westward. By this time lawmen were converging on the area in droves.

Near Newark, Perry's luck ran out. His engine ran out of steam and he had to abandon it. On foot he ran to a nearby farm house and under the threat of a gun stole a horse from the farmer. A short distance away the horse gave out and he was forced to steal another one. This time he not only got a horse but the sleigh with it. Stuck in an area unknown to him he found himself in Benton's Swamp. With his pursuers closing in on him he had no chose but to surrender.

OLIVER C. PERRY AS HE IS AND WAS. AND HIS CAPTORS.

His trial was set for May 1892, in Lyons. He reportedly told reporters that he would plead guilty to all charges and only secure the services of an attorney if charged with Attempted Murder for shooting McInerney. So, few were surprised when he was brought into the court room of Judge Rumsey and pled guilty to all charges. When Judge Rumsey asked if he wanted two days for respite, he replied "I have no reason to ask for respite as far as I am concerned." He then acknowledged that "I am Oliver Curtis Perry, born in Fulton County, am 26 years old, a carpenter by trade, not married, religious, read and write, have been convicted before and know no cause why the court should not pass sentence on me." With that said, Judge Rumsey sentenced Perry to 49 yrs. and 4 mos. of hard labor at Auburn Prison.

Perry's arrival in Auburn on Friday May 13, 1892, caused quite a commotion as hundreds gathered around the prison to catch a glimpse of the prisoner. Shackled and handcuffed he was accompanied by Wayne Co. Sheriff Walter Thornton, Under Sheriff George Jeffries, and Deputies "Ike" Reynolds and T.B. Trowbridge. Before turning Perry over to Auburn Prison officials, the Deputies took him off the train and brought him to the Home Restaurant just down the street from the State Street depot for dinner, delaying his admission for over an hour, much to the displeasure of Warden Charles Durston.

His stay at Auburn Prison wasn't without incident. He was a trouble maker who refused to work and was often confined to solitary. On Sunday October 23, 1892, he used the iron leg of his bed to dig out of his cell. Under the cover of darkness he crossed the prison yard and tried to enter the broom shop. Unable to gain entry he next tried the marble shop. Again, unable to gain entry he crossed the yard to the collar shop. However, this time he caught the attention of Keeper Titus who challenged him. When Perry refused to answer or appear Titus fired a shot over his head. Perry ran across the yard and right into the night stick of Keeper Smith. He was returned to solitary confinement. After spending only two years at Auburn, Warden Durston became concerned with Perry's continued strange and bad behavior and had Auburn Doctors Fredrick Sefton and Thomas Sawyer examine him. The two confirmed Perry was delusional and thought everyone was out to persecute and kill him. They declared him insane and arrangements were made to transfer him to Matteawan State Hospital.

But that wasn't going to be the last anybody ever heard of Perry. On the night of Friday April 12, 1895, Perry along with four other convicts escaped. On the run for five days he was apprehended in Weehawken, NJ. Dressed as a tramp and sitting with others around a camp fire near the rail yards he was taken into custody disheveled and broke. When Matteawan Keeper James Coyle showed up to escort him back to New York, Perry stated he would fight extradition "back to that treacherous hole." The two had a heated exchange as Perry swore vengeance on Coyle. He was eventually brought back to Matteawan.

In 1899, while still confined at Matteawan, he attempted to gain parole by sticking hot needles in both his eyes. The act blinded him and got him sent to Dannemora State Hospital for the Criminally Insane. At Dannemora, after a hunger strike also failed for a release, he somewhat settled down. He began a rigorous system of exercise and calisthenics and developed what was described as a "wonderful physique." He often wore only a loin cloth and never slept in a bed preferring the floor and even in the coldest weather had his window open. He also served as an arbitrator between prisoner disputes. He died at age 65 at Dannemora on Friday September 5, 1930 blind and insane. When his body went unclaimed he was buried in the prison cemetery.

NY Central American Express, similar to one robbed by Perry

Drawings of Matteawan State Hospital and cell block area showing location of escaped convicts cells as they appeared in newspaper

As an interesting side note....The five convicts escape from Matteawan created quite a sensation. Since all the men were confined in isolation many thought they must have had inside help. All were considered dangerous men and a reward was offered for their capture. NY Governor Levi Morton and the NY Central each offered a $1,000.00 just for the capture of Perry.

Frank Davis and Patrick McGuire (aka Ugly Mac) were from New York City, John Quigley was from Astoria and Michael O'Donnell was from Brooklyn. All the men had violent pasts and were serving time for burglary and grand larceny. McGuire had served time at Auburn and while confined there had made two previous escape attempts. He had also been involved in a previous escape plan at Matteawan but then had a change of heart and ratted out all those involved including a Keeper who was later arrested, tried and convicted for aiding and abetting a convict.

John Quigley was the first of the escapees to be apprehended. Two days after his escape he made the mistake of poking his head out of a freight car and asking a passing man if he had any food. The man, who thought Quigley may be one of the escapees, assured him he'd bring food back for him instead brought the law. Quigley upon his return to Matteawan gave a detailed account of the escape and much to everyone's surprise it wasn't Perry but McGuire who had masterminded it.

It seems McGuire had obtained impressions of the two keys needed to unlock the cell door, not from a Keeper but probably from a trustee allowed out of his cell for various duties and errands. With these impressions and two confiscated spoons he somehow was able to fashion the two keys needed to unlock the cells. Between checks on the night of the escape he exited his cell, unlocked the others and the men waited until Keeper William Carmody made another round. As Keeper Carmody entered the block the men, hidden in a darken corner, jumped him. As Carmody resisted, McGuire shouted "kill him," but Perry insisted "no don't do that, all we want is to get out of here." They stuffed Carmody's mouth with clothing, dragged him to McGuire's cell, tied him to the bed and took his keys. With Carmody's set of keys they exited the cell block and made their way to the chapel. Here, with the use of scaffolding left by workmen, they climbed to the ceiling, punched a hole through it and crawled out onto the roof. Making their way across the roof tops until they reached the front of the prison, they then shimmed down the eaves to the perimeter wall and jumped the remaining 20 feet to the ground. By the time they had reached the perimeter wall Carmody had managed to free himself and sounded the alarm. He even managed to fire one shot at the fleeing men as they jumped to the ground and fled into the dark. All of this didn't go un-noticed as an outside guard heard the commotion and fired three shots at them, all to no avail.

Once on the "outside" the men split up but their freedom was short lived. All were all caught, with the exception of Perry, within three days. Incidentally, Keeper William Carmody once resided in Auburn and was employed at Auburn Prison's Criminally Insane Asylum. He transferred to Matteawan when the Auburn Prison Asylum was closed.

THE SHELDON CASE

One of the most famous murders to have occurred in Cayuga County was committed on Jericho Road, in the Town of Brutus (now Sennett), way back on Thursday morning April 30, 1896. Perhaps because of the prominence of the murderer, his family and the unusual circumstances—was it suicide or murder—the investigation, arrest and trial became a front page news story in every paper in the state including New York City, where such things occur on a daily basis.

On aforesaid Thursday morning, the Sheldon family awoke, had breakfast and prepared for the day ahead. The two girls May and Jennie headed out to school while the two boys Guy and William headed out to the fields to work. Their father Frank prepared a buggy for a run to Jordan while his wife Eva Sheldon began her daily house chores. Their lives on the farm, in their small attractive house, had been good and they were all well liked and respected. But what was about to happen on this morning would change all their lives forever.

Frank returned from Jordan around 11:30am. When he entered the house he found his wife lying in the pantry. Rushing to her side he found that she was bleeding profusely from a head wound. His .32 caliber handgun laid a short distance from her body. He ran to the field and yelled to his sons "Your mother has committed suicide." The three returned to the house and placed her on the sofa. She was dead from what appeared to be a gunshot to her head. A messenger was sent for the authorities and Coroner Alvin Steward, of Port Byron.

MRS. EVA REMINGTON SHELDON

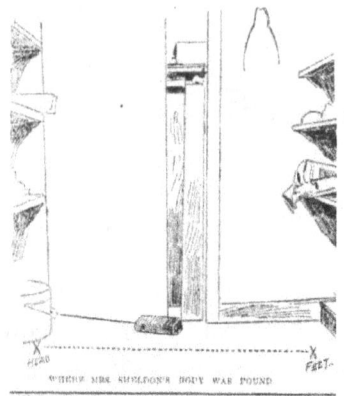
Scene of the murder as drawn in the newspaper.
Note the locations of the head & feet.

Doctor Fordyce Benedict, of Weedsport, assisted Coroner Steward with the autopsy. The two found Mrs. Sheldon had been shot approximately an inch behind and above her right ear, the bullet penetrating the skull into the brain. An inquest was conducted in Weedsport by Coroner Steward. District Attorney George Nellis represented the people while attorneys Robert Drummond (former DA) assisted by Weedsport attorney A.W. Shurtliff represented Frank Sheldon. During the course of the inquest, the District Attorney's office asked for the Court's permission to exhume Mrs. Sheldon's body so that a further expert examination of the head wound could be conducted. The Court approved the exhumation and on Wednesday May 20, 1896, Coroner-Doctor John Tripp, Doctors Eugene Foreman and Joseph Creveling along with ballistic expert Albert Hamilton conducted the examination at the grave site in the Weedsport Rural Cemetery. It is believed the prosecution is looking to prove that the handgun involved was not held close to the head as one would do when committing suicide but rather at a distance that would make it impossible for the deceased woman to hold the weapon and accomplish the shot to her head.

During the inquest, Hamilton testified that he found no burn marks or traces of lead or gun powder at the wound site. He stated that this proved the gun had been held at least 24" away from the head when it was fired, thus making it impossible for Mrs. Sheldon to hold the weapon and inflict the head shot. After a week and a half of testimony the jurors deliberated for forty minutes before returning their verdict.... "we find Eva Sheldon came to her death by means of a leaden bullet fired from a pistol in the hands of some person unknown." With that said Frank Sheldon was immediately arrested on a warrant, sworn out by Joseph Remington (the decease's brother), charging him with Murder First Degree. Although Frank was somewhat taken aback he showed no signs of agitation. He was taken before Justice L.B. Storke, arraigned and then taken to the County Jail. Although the verdict wasn't totally unexpected Sheldon's attorney A.W. Shurtliff wasn't satisfied with the decision. He stated "There was no reason for such a verdict. Either Mrs. Sheldon killed herself or Frank Sheldon killed her. No other person is responsible for her death and the jury should have either charged Sheldon directly with the crime or exonerated him from all blame."

FRANK SHELDON, THE ACCUSED HUSBAND.

Frank Sheldon's murder trial began in January 1897. DA Nellis prosecuted and attorneys Drummond and Shurtliff represented Sheldon. Justice James W. Dunwell presided. Spectators filled the court room every day. Quite a sensation was created when several witnesses, including two of Frank's children, testified that Sheldon was having an affair with his former house servant Ellen Sullivan, a woman described as comely and approximately 35 years old. Testimony from many witnesses was given that his affair with Sullivan continued even after she was let go and that he had been seen many times in her company at the Willard House, in Weedsport, where she was employed as a waitress. Further, that Frank left his home and family for several months, living in Michigan with Miss Sullivan, until early 1893 when he returned home and reunited with his family. However, witnesses testified the affair never ended and the two had been seen together as recently as the night before his wife's death. Spectators' ears perked when two residents of the Willard House testified they'd heard Miss Sullivan and Sheldon argue the night before Mrs. Sheldon's death. Miss Sullivan yelled at Frank "You haven't done as you agreed," to which he replied "I will if you give me time, I will when I get home." Then Miss Sullivan was heard yelling "I want you to leave right now and never come back," to which Sheldon was heard replying "Are you sure," and she replied "Yes, leave now."

As the trial progressed another sensation occurred when it was reported Miss Sullivan had left the Willard House and her whereabouts were unknown. A reporter from the Auburn Weekly Bulletin finally tracked her to

Auburn where he found her staying with her sister Mrs. Ellis Pulver at 15 Delevan Street. During a short interview with Miss Sullivan the reporter noted that she wasn't voluptuous nor graceful, that her hair wasn't quite blonde, her face was pale and thin, but that she was of gentle manner and quiet spoken. When asked if she thought Sheldon was guilty and had received a fair trial, she replied "I don't believe he killed his wife or that he had a fair trial." She denied that she was attending the trial daily in disguise. She stated although she read about it in the papers she had formed no opinion…."it is not for me to form an opinion." She stated "many of the witnesses have exaggerated everything about me" and that "Indeed, there had not been any such goings on. People that know me know that." She told the reporter that although she did not know where she would go, she would be leaving Auburn soon and would not be returning to Weedsport.

After several of Sheldon's friends and brothers testified on his behalf Frank Sheldon took the stand in his defense. He denied that he and Miss Sullivan were having an affair or that he ever had a sexual relationship with her. He denied that he loved her or had ever promised her that he would marry her. He said that he had never addressed a note or letter to Sullivan as "My Beloved Ellen." He stated that he had seen Miss Sullivan the night before his wife died but that they hadn't argued and parted on good terms. He admitted that there had been some martial difficulties and he left his wife and family in June of 1892 to live in Michigan. He stated since returning in February 1893 he and his wife had gotten along. He said the weapon used was his and it was usually kept in his bedroom. He continued by saying he believed his wife's continual health problems may have been why she committed suicide stating that "she suffered from pneumonia, congestive chills, grip, hay fever, aggravating spinal problems and constant headaches." He denied he had shot his wife and told the court that everyone that had testified against him hadn't told the truth.

The trial lasted seven weeks and the jury took 84 ½ hours before they finally announced they had a verdict. Twice they announced they were unable to come to a unanimous decision only to be sent back to the jury room. On Monday March 15, 1897, everyone was on edge when the jury announced they had found Sheldon guilty as charged. When asked by the Judge if he had anything to say before sentencing Sheldon replied "I am innocent of the crime charged." His attorneys moved for retrial which was denied. The Judge, after more arguments from the defense, then sentenced Sheldon to be confined to Auburn Prison until the week of April 25, 1897, when at the discretion of the Warden he be put to death in accordance with the laws of the State of New York.

Sheldon home as drawn in newspaper. Home still exists today.

As Sheldon spent his time in jail his attorneys fought to have the verdict overturned. The Court of Appeals eventually reversed the conviction. A second trial was begun on Monday February 27, 1899, only to be stopped when Sheldon hung himself at the County Jail on Thursday March 10, 1899. His funeral took place from the home of his brother former Assemblyman W. Clare Sheldon. He was forty-eight years old and was buried next to his wife in the Weedsport Rural Cemetery.

As an interesting side note....After Frank Sheldon's return from Michigan he was forced to sign a $2,000.00 bond promising to be faithful to his wife and family and support them to the best of his ability. The penalty for violating said bond was forfeiture of the money to his wife Eva, her heirs, executors or assignors. The bond was secured via W. Clare Sheldon and George Austin. Joseph V. Waldron and May B. Sheldon were appointed administrators. After his arrest and the rumors of Frank's continued affair with Miss Sullivan, the administrators filed a suit to recover the $2,000.00. Sheldon's attorney Robert Drummond kept the suit postponed on the plea it would prejudice the criminal trial. Upon Frank's death the suit was again scheduled to be heard in County Court. The suit was settled on Friday June 16, 1899. After expenses totaling $403.00 were deducted, each of the four Sheldon children would receive $399.25.

In 1995 author Donald J. Stinson wrote a wonderful book entitled *"Death In The Pantry,"* which delves much more into this fascinating story. The book is highly recommended by this author.

ANNIE EDSON TAYLOR
NIAGARA FALLS DAREDEVIL

Annie Edson Taylor was born in Auburn on Wednesday October 24, 1838. She was the daughter of Merrick and Lucretia (nee Waring) Edson. Her father owned a successful flour mill along the Owasco River which provided his family with more than enough to live a very comfortable life. Annie had three sisters and four brothers. She was educated in Auburn and although an active reader earned only average grades. She preferred to be outside playing boy's games than inside with the girls. Her father died when she was twelve years old but money he left for the family kept them financially stable and they continued to enjoy the life they'd come accustomed to.

After graduation she enrolled at the Conference Seminary and Collegiate Institute, in Charlotteville, NY. It was here she met, and at the age of seventeen, married David Taylor, of Branchport, NY. The couple had one son that died shortly after birth. Her husband was killed in action during the Civil War. At the age of twenty-five her life had changed quite drastically and she moved to San Antonio, Texas, to be near a friend. Having earned a degree she began a career teaching.

Annie spent many years traveling from school to school and eventually ended up returning to New York., where she studied dance. She became a dancing instructor and ended up in Bay City, Michigan. With her inheritance money running low she saw an opportunity to make money by opening a dance school. Because of her high life she bought quality high end furnishings and supplies for her new dance studio. She eventually was spending more money running the school than she was taking in. The school ran into financial difficulties and closed. For the next few years she moved quite frequently and lived in Mexico City, Mexico, Chattonoogna, Birmingham, San Francisco, Washington, DC, Chicago, Indianapolis and even Syracuse, NY. She ended up in Sault Ste. Marie, on Michigan's upper peninsula, where she taught music.

All of these years of traveling and missed opportunities at a successful career were quickly eating through the money in her savings account. By May of 1900, she was back in Bay City. In August of 1901, while reading a newspaper article on the Pan-American Exposition being held in Buffalo, NY, an idea came to her of how to earn a lot of money. Realizing how many people were flocking to Buffalo and nearby Niagara Falls, she would take advantage of the crowds by being promoting herself as the first person to successfully ride in a barrel over Niagara Falls. Many had swam across the river and many others had shown their skills crossing the Falls on a tight rope but no one had ever gone over it and survived. She believed her idea would bring her fame and fortune.

Annie began by contacting several area barrel makers, but many refused to be a part of her suicidal plan. Finally, the West Bay City Cooperage Co., agreed to construct her specially designed barrel. The barrel, made of oak and wrapped with steel bands was four feet in length, three feet in diameter and weighed 160 pounds. A 100 pound anvil was also placed on the bottom of the barrel for ballast, ensuring the barrel's top would remain floating upright. Cushioning was placed all around the inside and straps to secure Annie in place were added. Strapping was also placed on the outside so hooks for retrieving it could catch it once it went over the falls and down river. Once all this was accomplished she contacted well known Bay City promoter Frank M. "Tussy" Russell. After an agreement and contract with Russell was made he began promoting the daredevil stunt, at first only saying an unnamed person was about to engage in going over Niagara Falls in barrel. In September of 1901, her specially designed barrel was put on display in the window of Smith and Purser's Department Store, in Bay City. In early October Russell headed to Niagara Falls with the barrel and began promoting the upcoming stunt there. The Police Chiefs on both sides of the boarder warned Russell that he would be held criminally liable if Annie was killed. He consulted with his attorneys who advised him "not to worry about it."

On Saturday October 12th., Annie hopped a train and headed to Niagara Falls. At the station she told reporters "I might as well be dead as to remain in my present condition." When a reporter asked if she was contemplating suicide she replied "Not by any means. I am a good Epsicoplian to do such a thing as that. I believe in a *Supreme Ruler* and fully realize what self destruction would mean in the *Hereafter*." The reporter then asked what put this suicidal idea into your head, Annie replied "It is not a suicidal idea with me. I entertain the utmost confidence that I shall succeed in going over the Falls without any harm resulting to me."

On Tuesday October 22, 1901, in Niagara Falls, NY, a crowd gathered as Russell had a cat named Lagara placed in the barrel. The barrel was then towed out onto the Niagara River about a mile above the falls and released. Approximately twenty minutes the barrel was located intact downstream of the falls and secured. Brought to shore and opened many were surprised that the cat survived.

On Thursday October 24th., as a large crowd gathered on both sides of Niagara Falls and along the river Annie boarded a small boat and with the barrel in tow was rowed about two miles upstream from the Falls. It was also her 63rd. birthday.

Annie, dressed in a long black gown and fashionable hat and with her lucky heart shaped pillow climbed into the barrel. Her assistants begged her not to attempt the stunt but she was so confident of success she ignored their pleads and told them to secure the lid. Once the lid was in place and secured air was pumped into the barrel by a bicycle pump. With everything in order the barrel was cut loose….it was 405pm. She was now at the mercy of the river that never before had been known to spare a human life. The river's strong current quickly carried it down river towards Horseshoe Falls on the Canadian side.

As thousands of spectators watched the barrel bobbing downstream toward the falls it would occasionally disappear in the rapids. Many believed they were watching a suicidal disaster. Within two minutes it had reached its destination and over the brink of Horseshoe Falls it descended the 167 foot drop and disappeared in the white capped churning waters and mist at the bottom of the falls.

Within a minute the barrel appeared again upright and floating. Crews quickly rowed out to retrieve it. At 420pm, the barrel was brought ashore and opened. Carlisle Graham called out to Annie and when he heard her reply "Where am I," he yelled out "My God she's still alive." Annie exited the barrel stunned and bruised but she had survived and became the first person to ever conquer Niagara Falls in a barrel. Asked what it was like, she replied "No one ought ever do that again."

She later told reporters "I prayed ever second I was in the barrel except for a few seconds after the fall when I went unconscious."

Annie, her cat Lagara and her barrel

Her name was splashed across newspaper headlines around the world. For a while speaking engagements, autographs and pictures of her and her barrel brought in some monies. But as that began to dry up her promoter Frank Russell absconded with her barrel forcing her to use much of her savings hiring private detectives to find it. It was eventually found in Chicago and returned. She had achieved the fame but not the fortune she so wanted and desired. She continued on with occasional speaking engagements and selling pictures and autographs from her home in Lockport, NY.

Annie died poor at the age of 82 on Friday April 29, 1921 at the Niagara County Infirmary. She is buried at Oakwood Cemetery in Niagara Falls, NY.

Since Annie's successful stunt at least fifteen others have rode over the falls in barrels, inner tubes and even a jet ski. Some weren't as fortunate as Annie and didn't survive their trip. Thus a not so well known Auburnian became the first person to conquer Niagara Falls.

HERMAN BARTELS SR. AND THE OLD FANNING BREWING CO.

In 1904, the former Fanning Brewery, located on Garden Street was sold at foreclosure to prominent Syracusian Herman Bartels Sr., owner of Bartels Brewing Co., in that city. Mr. Bartels paid $16,500.00 for the building and contents. He then sold a house and a lot on the property for $4,500.00, making the total price paid $12,000.00. Monroe Brewing had been using the building for storage. Mr. Bartels will continue to use the building for Monroe and his Lake Shore Brewing Co., both subsidiaries of his Syracuse business. All this good news would soon turn into bad particularly for Mr. Bartels.

HERMAN BARTELS.

But first a little background on Herman Bartels Sr.. As a young man, he spent three years as a brewer's apprentice before coming to the States from Germany in 1872 at the age of 19. He quickly found work at the NY State Brewery, in Auburn, where he worked for three years before moving to Cincinnati. There he partnered with others in the brewery business. He returned to New York and settled in Syracuse where he obtained work as a brew master at Haberie Brewing Co. and later at Germania Brewing Co.. He held interests in the Central NY Pottery Co., in Chittenango, the Syracuse Cold Storage Warehouse Co., and two other breweries located in Elmira and Rochester. Quite successful he was finally able to wrestle a majority of the stock control of the Germania Brewing Co. and changed its name to Bartels Brewing Co.

Now for the rest of the story. On Tuesday September 13, 1904, Patrick Connors, of West Street, walked to the old Fanning Brewery, on Garden Street, to meet with his brother-in-law John Lawler. Lawler was working at the old plant as the managing agent for Monroe Brewery which was using the space for storage. When he entered the office Lawler wasn't there.

As Patrick began looking around the building for John he began smelling a strong odor of kerosene and oil. He noticed that the floors and walls seemed to be drenched in the substances. When he checked the cooler he saw a barrel of oil that appeared to have been dumped onto the sprinklers. He then thought he heard two men talking up on the second floor but when he tried the trap door to the second floor he found it weighted down. He next checked the door to the living quarters, attached to the brewery, but found it nailed shut and a door on the south malt house had a new padlock on it. However, on the north side of the malt house he was able to gain entry to the upper floors. Upon reaching the second floor, he noticed that several holes had been haphazardly hacked into the floor and several barrels of oil and kerosene appeared to have been spilled about. Since he hadn't located John or anyone else, he decided to walk to John's home at 84 South Street to inform him of what he'd found. When he reached the corner of Garden and North Streets he found John headed his way. Informing him of what he had seen the two men returned to the old plant and began looking around. What they found looked quite suspicious, several barrels of oil and kerosene had been dumped. The two substances saturated the floors and walls on all five floors of the building. Kindling and old rags saturated with both substances had been placed about and holes had been punched through all the floors. Oil drenched lines of rope ran from floor to floor through each of the holes to the piles of the old rags and kindling. Other combustible materials had been scattered about. An exposed electrical line ran from its on/off switch to one of these drenched rag piles. Doors and windows that had been shut and locked were now open. As they continued their inspection, they heard voices coming from the fourth floor.

On the fourth floor they encountered John Dippold and Martin Whitting. Both men were from Syracuse but Lawler had seen them in the plant before and knew they'd been employed by Bartels. When he asked what they were doing Dippold replied "I don't believe it's any of your business." Taking exception to that John told the two men that they had better leave. Dippold started down the stairs as John and Patrick followed. Upon reaching the offices on the first floor John asked Dippold where Whitting had gone to. Dippold replied "I'll go get him," and he returned to the upper floors. John then phoned Herman Bartels Sr. and informed him of what he had found and his suspicions that someone was planning to burn the building down. When Dippold returned, without Whitting, John was still on the phone with Mr. Bartels. Bartels asked to speak with Dippold, their conversation was short, and then Dippold quickly left. Meanwhile, Patrick had left to inform the Police of what they'd found.

Officer Norman Parker returned with Patrick and inspected the plant. Surprised at what he found, he summoned the Detectives and Chief William Bell. Police were immediately suspicious of what they found and wanted to speak with Dippold and Whitting. However, by that time both men had disappeared. Syracuse authorities were notified to be on the lookout for the two.

When Auburn Detectives spoke with Herman Bartels Sr., he readily admitted that he knew both Dippold and Whitting as former disgruntled employees. He stated that both men had recently been at the plant cleaning and painting old beer kegs. He told Police that he hadn't seen either of the men recently and had no idea where they had gone. He also admitted that the plant and its contents were insured for between $60,000.00 and $75,000.00. This fact made Police very suspicious that there may have been a plot to destroy the building and then collect a large insurance settlement, particularly since Bartels had only paid $12,000.00 for the property. They began to wonder if Bartels himself was involved.

Months went by and Police were no closer to finding either Dippold or Whitting. Finally, Auburn Mayor Thomas Osborne stepped forward and hired the Metropolitan Detective Agency, of Chicago to pursue the two men. They in turn put Private Investigator E.M. Buckminster on the case. Buckminster almost immediately tracked the two men to New Jersey, where he learned they had separated. He learned that Dippold had headed to Connecticut while Whitting headed south. Buckminster next tracked Dippold to Canada and then to Brantfold, Ontario. Kept under surveillance for several days, Buckminster took Dippold into custody when Dippold crossed the border and traveled to Chicago. He brought Dippold back to Auburn on Sunday April 30, 1905. Whitting remained a fugitive, his whereabouts unknown.

Dippold's return to Auburn was kept low key. Police didn't want to tip their hand if others were involved in the arson plot. On Tuesday September 13th., Dippold provided a full confession as to his activities at the old Fanning Brewery. What he told Police and District Attorney Robert Burritt was what they had been thinking all along.

Dippold stated that he and Martin Whitting, of Solvay, had been hired by William O'Hara, of Syracuse, to burn the old brewery down. That O'Hara was acting on the orders of Herman Bartels Sr., and had supplied them with the money to acquire the materials to do the job. He stated that Whittings' wife Margaret assisted with obtaining the oil and kerosene and both she and O'Hara helped make the arrangements to get the substances to Auburn.

JOHN DIPPOLD.

He stated after John Lawler discovered him and Whitting in the building and phoned Bartels Sr., he got on the phone and told Bartels that they had been discovered and he was unable to carry out their plan. He said that Bartels told him to come to Syracuse immediately. He stated that he and Whitting immediately left Auburn via train and went to Bartels home in Syracuse. Although they were unable to meet with Bartels that night, they met with him and O'Hara the following day in Camillus where they were hiding out with friends. Dippold stated that Bartels suggested that he and Whitting leave the state before Police found them and the whole plot was exposed. When both men hesitated, Bartels gave them money to leave and told them he would have an attorney contact them. They took the money and headed to New Jersey. Dippold continued... while in Jersey they learned that an investigator was on their trail so they split up. He said that he headed to Connecticut and Whitting headed south. He told investigators that over the next several months, while on the run and hiding out in Canada, he had met three or four times with Bartels' attorney Edward Shannahan who supplied him with money and clothing.

With Dippold's statement, the Police had what they needed to obtain arrest warrants for Martin Whitting, his wife Margaret, William O'Hara and Herman Bartels Sr.. On Monday evening May 1st., with the newly acquired warrants in hand, Chief William Bell, Acting Capt. Norman Parker, Officers William O'Dea and Patrick Graney headed to Syracuse on the 9:50pm train. By the time the Coppers reached Syracuse they had little trouble rounding up their suspects who were all caught at their homes asleep. The first arrest at 2:40am was Herman Bartels Sr.. By 5:00am the Police had three of the suspects in custody and were able to make the 6:50am train back to Auburn. The suspects were accompanied by Syracuse attorneys Edward Shannahan and Andrew Cowie and George McGuire, district agent for United States Fidelity & Guaranty Co., who was expected to post the bonds for the defendants. All the defendants were brought before Recorder Stupp charged with Attempted Arson Third Degree. They all pled not guilty. Bail was set at $3,000.00 for Bartels Sr. and $2,000.00 each for Dippold, O'Hara and Margaret Whitting.

Herman Bartels Senior's trial began on Monday April 9, 1906, in Cayuga County Court before Judge A.H. Searing. He was represented by Auburn attorneys Hull Greenfield and Frank Cady. District Attorney Burritt was assisted by ADA Frank Coburn. The defense's first move was an attempt to have the trial moved out of the City of Auburn. The judge ruled against it.

The star witness for the prosecution was John Dippold who retold his version of the events as he had in his statement. Mr. Bartels also testified. He stated that Dippold and Whitting were blackmailing him, "I was afraid of them and thought it better to allow myself to be blackmailed. I gave them money and clothing out of fear." He also produced a witness that allegedly heard the two men discuss their intent to frame the "old man" (referring to

Bartels Sr.) if they got caught. This witness, a man from New Jersey, told the court that Dippold had informed him that he and Whitting were stealing from the old plant and planned on burning it to destroy evidence. Further, that if they were caught they planned on "blaming the old man." Other witnesses included William O'Hara, Margaret Whitting and Mary Dippold. The two wives testified to the fact that they had both received money either directly from Bartels or an intermediate. Mrs. Dippold stated Bartels offered to give her $500.00 and buy her a home in Canada if she would leave and join her husband there. O'Hara, who still maintained his innocence, stated that on Bartels orders he had provided money and clothing to both Dippold and Whitting but had no idea that any of them were plotting to burn the brewery. Even attorney Edward Shannon was called to the stand. He also related how he'd met with both Dippold and Whitting and provided them with money and clothing via Bartels. He stated that his meetings with Dippold were while he was on the run in Connecticut and Canada. He stated he acted on behalf of Bartels but had no idea that any of the defendants were plotting arson.

The trial lasted three weeks and there were many heated arguments between the opposing attorneys. In the end it took the jury just over eight hours to convict Bartels as charged. Bartels took the news well although he admitted that he thought he would be acquitted. His bail was continued until sentencing on April 30th.. On Monday April 30th., all involved parties, except Bartels, were present for his sentencing. As his attorneys and the Police checked on his location it became apparent that he had fled. District Attorney Burritt moved that Bartels' bond be revoked and a warrant be issued for him. In October 1906, Bartels' bondsman settled with Cayuga County and paid $6,000.00.

In April 1907, Canadian authorities located Bartels living high at the Clifton Hotel in Niagara Falls, Ontario. The hotel was described as one of Niagara Falls finest. Bartels denied he was the man wanted in Auburn but when told Auburn authorities were en-route he quickly admitted that he was in fact the man they wanted. Although Canadian authorities arrested Bartels Auburn authorities soon learned that Canada would not extradite him on the arson charges. DA Burritt moved quickly to have Bartels indicted for Purjury.

May 1907 was a busy month for Bartels. While being held in a Canadian jail his extradition hearing on the Perjury charge began. However, Bartels had other plans. On Thursday July 4th., he escaped. His freedom was cut short when he was recaptured on Monday July 16th.. While on the run, his money ran out, he lost weight and suffered a mild stroke. When he appeared in Court on an escape charge he appeared haggard. He was sentenced to 90 days in the jail's medical ward due to paralysis of the right side of his face. He was returned to Auburn on November 3rd.. On Tuesday March 3, 1908, Bartels was sentenced to serve one year and two months in Auburn Prison. He was released on Monday May 11, 1909. He told reporters that "my work in the prison broom shop had kept me busy during the day but the nights were oh so very hard." He said he had business plans but would wait until after he had taken a fishing vacation at Brewerton to make any announcements. His son who arrived by car to pick up his father, arrived too late and Bartels caught the train back to Syracuse accompanied by his architect and contactor.

Thus, the saga of Herman Bartels Senior's five year involvement with the old Fanning Brewing Company and one of Auburn's longest drawn out criminal cases ended.

As an interesting side note....Bartels eventually lost ownership of the Fanning building via bankruptcy. The building was later used as a cold storage facility, a tire and auto accessory store, and a fruit and procedure warehouse/store. Parts of the building still exist today occupied by Trombley's Auto Service and Advantage Auto Supply.

Martin Whitting was eventually located living with his family in Winnipeg, Manitoba, Canada. He was never brought back to Auburn to answer to the charge of Arson.

FRONTENAC BURNS, EIGHT DIE

Soon after Robert Fulton and his steamboat The Clermont made a successful voyage up the Hudson River, from New York City to Albany, on August 17, 1807, the steamboat industry took off. By 1820 many other entrepreneurs began using steamboats to transport passengers, freight and the US mail along America's rivers and lakes. Cayuga Lake was no exception and by 1842 a Timothy D. Wilcox had moved to Ithaca and bought up the Cayuga Lake Steamboat Company. Mr. Wilcox was no stranger to the steamboat industry. He had worked as a deck hand on Fulton's steamboats and had captained Long Island Sound steamers before coming to Ithaca. Under Captain Wilcox's guidance the company was quite successful and he commissioned several new steamers such as the Kate Morgan, Sheldrake and the T.D. Wilcox, which he named after himself. This steamer provided complete service such as regular meals and a full orchestra for entertainment.

Although the company exchanged ownership several times by 1870 Wilcox again owned the company. That year he commissioned the building of the largest steamer to ply Cayuga Lake's waters....The Frontenac. Fifty thousand dollars was spent to build the 135 foot long "side-wheeler," with a 22 foot beam between the inside casings for the paddlewheels and a 270HP engine capable of 17mph which for those days was considered quite fast. The ship could accommodate as many as 350 people in her cabins, dining room and decks. The Frontenac made its maiden voyage on Friday June 24, 1870. It was Wilcox's pride and he personally piloted it until his death in 1884. Four years after his death, his wife and daughter sold the company to the Cayuga Lake Transportation Company. They continued to run the company until 1902 when Captain Melvin P. Brown, of Syracuse bought the company.

Captain Brown, along with his two sons Clarence and Howard, operated the Brown Transportation Company. They added their old Onondaga Lake steamers Mohawk, Iroquois and Commander to their Cayuga fleet and Brown's sons captained these steamers. By the time Brown bought the company, the Frontenac had been sailing on Cayuga Lake for 32 years. He invested $5,000.00 to up-grade the Frontenac, rebuilding parts of the wooden structure and installing new boilers.

The Frontenac would leave Ithaca at 900am and head north to Cayuga. It made several stops along the eastside of the lake and would make the 50 mile trip to Cayuga by 115pm. It would leave Cayuga by 315pm, make stops along the Westside of the lake and return to Ithaca at 810pm. Captain Brown personally captained the Frontenac and his wife worked in the kitchen.

On Friday July 26, 1907, the Frontenac was on a special excursion and spent the night in Cayuga. At 845am the next morning it set off from Cayuga and headed to Sheldrake, on the Westside of the lake, to meet the Mohawk so passengers could be exchanged. After making the exchange the Frontenac crossed to the eastside of the lake and began its trip north with approximately 60 passengers aboard. Along with Captain Brown, his wife and five crewmen they found a strong northwest wind blowing and the lake quite choppy. Later reports stated there were gales up to 50mph and waves as high as six feet.

The conditions prevented Frontenac from making its scheduled stops at Levanna and Aurora.

The Frontenac burning as drawn in the papers

At 100pm the Frontenac was in the middle of the lake, approximately a thousand feet from shore, as it neared Farley's Point. Many campers along the shore could see there was a fire on the ship. On board the ship, twelve year old Roland Genung ran to Captain Brown and told him that there was a fire on the upper deck. Brown immediately ran to the upper deck and began searching. It didn't take long before he found a fire near the crank pit, forward of the boiler room. He immediately ran to engineer Howard Bachman, informing him there was a fire he ordered that the water pumps be turned on. Once this was done Brown ran back to the fire, turned on the fire hoses and began fighting the fire. By this time most passengers realized there was a fire, but felt it was nothing to worry about and that it would be quickly extinguished. Seeing that he was making little progress, the fire was growing larger as the strong wind fanned it, Brown ordered Pilot Albert E. Smith to head toward shore as fast as he could.

By the time the ship was beached at Dill's Cove, approximately 200 feet from shore, the fire was raging and eating away at the upper deck and stern. Many of the life boats could no longer be reached. The blaze and smoke could be seen for miles. As the crew began passing out life jackets many of the passengers began jumping into the water. Others too frightened to jump were assisted into the water by the crew. People along the shore grabbed whatever they could to assist the men, women and children in the water. As few boats were available, some men on shore swam out to rescue those passengers flailing about in the high waves that kept pushing them back against the burning boat and making it almost impossible to swim toward shore. Women wearing long skirts were having a particularly difficult time in the water as their skirts became watered down and heavy they were unable to swim or keep above water. Once Captain Brown was sure all passengers and crew were safely off the burning vessel he also jumped into the water and swam to shore.

Many of the passengers praised Brown, his crew members and the campers and farmers who had come to their rescue. They also spoke about some of the cowardly acts they had witnessed by a few men passengers who had only looked out for their own safety. One passenger related how one man, who was wearing a life jacket, upon reaching shore offered $500.00 cash to anyone who would return to the burning boat to rescue his wife.

When news of the disaster reached Auburn, several Auburn physicians along with Coroner Lewis F. O'Neill boarded a special Lehigh Valley Railroad train that was dispatched to the scene with medical supplies. Sheriff George S. Fordyce and District Attorney Robert J. Burritt also went to the scene.

Many of the passengers that were lucky enough to have been rescued or make it to shore on their own had been burned. They were treated and attended to by those on shore who had seen the burning ship and rushed to help. Rescuers continued to search for survivors but as the hours passed only bodies were found. In all eight passengers died:

1) Miss Julia C. McCreary, from Cohoes, NY
2) Miss Estella Clinton, from Ithaca, NY
3) Mrs. Lena Genung, wife of Dr. Homer Genung, Freeville, NY
4) Carl Genung, her 4 yr. old son
5) Miss Alida Bennett, from Frankfort, NY
6) Grace Adel, age 6, from Trumansburg, NY
7) Miss Eva Mott, from Port Alleghany, NY
8) Miss Marietta Sullivan, from Syracuse, NY

The Frontenac continued to burn into the night until most of it was burnt to water level. On Sunday morning all that could be seen of the mighty steamer were the smoldering twisted ruins of its engine, boilers and battered paddlewheel protruding from the lake in approximately six feet of water.

That morning Coroner O'Neill used the Union Springs Town Hall to conduct his investigation into the fire and deaths. O'Neill had secured many of the passengers' testimony during his investigation Saturday. Much of Sunday was used for the testimony of the ship's crew. Pilot Smith, Engineer Bachman, deckhands Roland Brown, Edward Saunders and Wayland

Hollenbeck all testified. Captain Brown's testimony was taken late in the day and was the last received.

On Monday July 28, 1907, Coroner O'Neill stated all of the deaths were the result of drowning. He exonerated the captain and his crew from any and all blame. He stated "they were brave, cool headed fellows and did far more under all the circumstances than many others would have done. They are not only entitled to exoneration but the highest praise." He also noted that the cause of the fire could not be determined by examination of the passengers and crew. D.A. Burritt and Sheriff Fordyce stated there would be no criminal investigation or charges brought.

As an interesting side note....the press called the incident "a disaster" and the deaths of six women and two children a tragedy. Miss Marietta Sullivan, age 30, was employed as a stenographer at the Syracuse law firm of Gannon, Spencer & Michell. She had spent a few days with friends at Sheldrake and was en-route to Cayuga to meet her fiancé Willis Michell. Her body was the last to be found. It was noted at 600pm, Arthur Post was searching the scene in his small motorboat named Minnie when its propeller suddenly and abruptly stopped. When Post checked he found something wrapped tightly around the prop. Upon further inspection he found Miss Sullivan's body under his boat, her hair tangled around the propeller. Not wanting to take a chance on harming the young woman's body any further he was towed to shore where he and a few other men lifted Sullivan's body out of the water and onto shore. Her head had been badly cut and her face was badly disfigured by the propeller. As the men laid her with the dead one of them placed a cloth over her face. As all that was happening Willis Michell arrived at the Auburn station and learned of the Frontenac burning on Cayuga Lake. He quickly obtained a ride to the scene and looked for Marietta. Unable to find her among the survivors he was directed to the dead. He identified her body not by looking at her face but by the diamond engagement ring on her finger. He told the Sheriff not to remove the cloth covering her face...."I do not want to see her in that condition."

For several years the wreck site remained a huge tourist attraction as literally thousands boated to the site or stood along the shore to get a glimpse. Eventually the campers at Dill's Cove and Farley's Point, along with the State, wanted the debris removed. This was finally accomplished in 1917. Due to the shortage of iron caused by World War One, most of the ship's iron was salvaged for use during the war.

Captain Brown planned on building a new steamer to replace the Frontenac but that never happened. The development of faster railroads able to haul more freight and passengers, along with the automobile and modern roads, signaled the beginning of the end for the steamers. Captain Brown continued captaining tugs along the Erie Canal until his death at Port Byron on Friday September 15, 1922, behind the wheel of his tugboat "Allen." He was 72 years old and is buried in Riverside Cemetery, in Baldwinsville, NY.

Two of Brown's ships, Iroquois and Mohawk as seen on postcards:

GEORGE E. CARR
(and a remarkable family history)

George E. Carr was born in Union Springs, NY, on November 3, 1840. He was a decedent of the Carr family, one of the first pioneer families to settle along the eastern shore of Cayuga Lake, just south of Union Springs, while the native Cayuga Indians were still residing there. Mr. Carr married Emily Anthony and they had two children, a son Wallace and a daughter Maude.

George was well known throughout the area as an expert wood carver and fine musician, having played in many area bands and orchestras. When the Civil War broke out he enlisted in the 19th. NY Infantry and served in the Company's band. When the band was discharged on orders of the War Department he enlisted in the Navy and served aboard the USS Lancaster until October 24, 1865.

Sometime after the War he moved his family to Barber's Corners, in the Town of Ledyard and it is here where he became famous for his Totem Tree.

In 1911, when an old maple tree died on his front lawn, George began carving figures upon its trunk and limbs. First was the bust of a woman's head followed quickly by a wide variety of animals, birds, reptiles and bird houses. In all there are 40 figures all painted in their natural tint....an elephant, lion, dog, monkey, gorilla, owl, snake, hippo, an American eagle and even an alligator.

After just about every available spot on the tree's surface was covered with carvings Mr. Carr turned his genius to other trees and curious stone formations. As the fame of his handiwork spread thousands of sightseers from all over the country would visit the property while the motoring season was open.

In July 1926 a terrible summer storm demolished the famous Totem Tree. Blown over by high winds and so decayed little was left of the tree. George died at the age of 86 on Sunday December 5, 1926. He was survived by his wife, son, daughter and brothers Norman and Fred. He is buried in Evergreen Cemetery in Scipioville.

As an interesting side note....while doing research on George E. Carr and his Totem Tree, I came across an interesting article written in the June 13, 1905 edition of the paper concerning the Carr family of Union Springs. Written by Jonathan Carr the article reports that the Carr family had been involved in every war the United States had ever been in up until that time (1905).

He began his article with James Carr Sr., who was born in Londonderry, New Hampshire. James was 27 years old when the Revolutionary War began in 1775 and he enlisted in the Continental Army. During the war he became familiar with the Cayuga Lake region while serving with Colonel William Butler as they laid waste to Indian villages along the east side of the lake during what became known as the Sullivan and Clinton Campaign. On October 10, 1780, at the battle of Fort Ann, he was taken prisoner by the British and held for two years in Montreal, Canada. James also served as a Captain during the French and Indian Wars. After his discharge he resided in Johnstown, NY with his wife and six children. For his service during the war he was given a land grant of 1,600 acres. Familiar with Cayuga Lake and its fertile land he chose property just south of Union Springs that is now known as Carr's Cove. He befriended the Cayuga Indians that were still residing in the area and for three years he traveled between his home in Johnstown and his lake property before moving his family to the "Cove." Here he raised four more children. James Sr. had ten children in all, six boys and four girls.

He died on Wednesday May 3, 1839 and is buried in the old Quaker Cemetery in Union Springs.

Alexander Carr was the son of James Sr. He was born in Johnston, NY on Tuesday September 24, 1793 and was a soldier on the Niagara Frontier during the War of 1812. He took part in the Battle of Chippawa and the sortie against Fort Erie. His two sons James and William served during the Civil War.

Jacob Carr, Alexander's brother, was also born in Johnstown. He also served during the War of 1812 at the Battle of Chippawa and the sortie of Fort Erie. His two grandsons, George and Norman Carr, served during the Civil War. Jacob is buried in the old Quaker Cemetery in Union Springs.

Albert Carr, the son of Jonathan Carr, served as a Second Lieutenant in the 19th. NY Infantry during the Civil War.

Hartman Carr's four sons all served during the Civil War-- Ashbel, was a private in the 19th. NY Infantry, Henry C., also a private with the 19th. NY Infantry, Hartman Jr., served with the Navy and Jonathan was a Captain with Co. 1, 1st. Ohio Cavalry.

Daniel W. Carr, son of James Sr., was a bugler with General Winfred Scott's Headquarters. He part took in the siege and capture of Vera Cruz and Mexico City.

Residence of Henry C. Carr, Carrs Cove, Cayuga Lake, N. Y.

James Carr Jr.'s two sons Lafayette and George served in the Civil War with the 19th. NY Infantry and the 3rd. Artillery. Both were captured in action and sent to the notorious Confederate prisoner camp at Andersonville, Georgia where they both died.

To this day the Cayuga Lake property that the Carr family lived on for so long is known as Carr's Cove. The Carr family continued to honorable serve its Country in the years and wars that followed. A truly remarkable family indeed.

A HORSE THIEF, A CAR THIEF AND A DARING JAIL ESCAPE

At 600am Wednesday morning September 4, 1912, Cayuga County Jailor Frank McDowell had just finished serving inmates their breakfast when he noted he had two meals left over. Frank knew this wasn't right and an immediate count of the inmates was begun. Within minutes the Jail staff realized two inmates, James Blake and Otis Comfort, were missing. As a lock down and search of the facility began Jailors soon realized the two missing inmates had somehow managed to escape.

During the search McDowell found a hole had been cut through an old iron heating grate which had served as a register in the cell block. The perforated iron grate was three quarters of an inch thick and the hole sawed through it was 16 1/2" long by 9" wide. Through this small hole the two inmates were able to drop down into the basement where McDowell then discovered two iron bars covering an eastside basement window had also been cut through making an opening approximately 10" by 11". Near the window McDowell found three small saws.

Sheriff George Bancroft was immediately notified and he along with Deputy Tom Walker started out on the chase in the Sheriff's car. Under Sheriff John Drake got busy notifying all area Police agencies as an APB was issued. As McDowell began questioning inmates he soon ran up against the old inmate code of "mum's the word." None of them was "gonna rat out their departed lodgers." McDowell found one trusty who would only say "Frank, you don't see the alarm clock hanging on the wall, do you?"

What was left of the old clock was found in Blake's cell. The clock, which had hung on the wall for a decade, had been dismantled. The cons had taken the clock's springs, tempered them over a gas plate until they were rigid enough to be crafted into small saws. A lot of time and planning went into the escape. It was obvious the two cons had spent several nights working on their escape. Jailors stated after a 1000pm check no one is left on duty at the jail as it was believed no one could escape from the heavily wired and ironed sealed cell block. Jailer McDowell stated when he made the 1000pm check all inmates were present and everything appeared to be in order.

The first clues of the escapees' whereabouts started coming in around 800am. Several farmers in the Fleming area reported attempts to get into their barns had been made. Finally, Frank Casler of South Street Road, Fleming, reported sometime after midnight his mare and buggy had been stolen from the barn of Patrick Welsh near the Sand Beach Cemetery. The mare was described as a dark bay with a white spot on its forehead, 15 ½ hands high. The buggy has a dark top, black body with red running gear, automobile seat and rubber tires. Shortly after Casler's report another report came in from Moravia that two men matching the escapees' description had passed through the village in a buggy at 700am. Deputy Fay Teeter of Moravia took up the search of roads south of the village.

The Sheriff's Office reports James Blake, is 26 years old, 135 pounds, slim build, light complexion and freckled face, last seen wearing a blue suit of clothes. Otis Comfort is 25 years old, 155 pounds, 5'08", brown hair and light complexion, last seen wearing a brown suit of clothes. Blake was arrested in Syracuse for the May 19th. theft of a car belonging to Charles Kanaley, of Weedsport, from the Lakeside Park grounds. Deputies report Blake is from Detroit and a mechanic. They believe he was responsible for making the saws used in the escape. Comfort was arrested in Springport May 1st. for the theft of a horse and buggy belonging to William Grant, of Sennett. He had been employed on Grant's farm and was in possession of the horse and buggy when arrested. Deputies report he is from Elmira and believe he was en-route home when apprehended. He had served time in both Elmira and Auburn Prisons for horse theft. The pair made a fine combination as Blake has knowledge of tools, such as those made for the escape, and Comfort has experience with entering a barn and making off with a horse.

Both men were confined to County Jail awaiting action by the October Grand Jury. Sheriff Bancroft issued a $50.00 reward per man.

With the announcement of the reward many new leads started coming in from all over the County. People in Fair Haven reported seeing two suspicious men and calls came in from Weedsport, Union Springs and Cayuga. Sam Cooper, of 17 West Street, Auburn told Auburn City Police while driving into Auburn earlier in the morning he'd seen two men get out of buggy near Oakwood. He said as he approached the two men they took up positions in the roadway in an attempt to get him to stop. He stated the two men acted like they may have had guns but as he drew nearer to them he could see it was a bluff. Cooper said he was alone with no means to protect himself so he gunned up his auto and sped pass the two men who in turn quickly jumped out of harm's way to the side of the road.

Another man by the name of Harris, from Victory, told Police that he'd just learned of the escape upon reaching Auburn. He told the coppers that around dusk Wednesday evening he'd been out searching for some cattle that had gotten loose when his attention was drawn to some smoke rising above the trees in a wooded area just outside of town. He said as he approached the wooded area he saw two young men cooking over a small fire. Harris said he was about to check on the two men when he heard his cattle nearby and wanting to get them in before it got too dark he paid no more attention to the two men. Harris, who is a pretty good sized muscular man, stated if he'd known of the escape at the time he would have brought the two in. He was pretty sure they were the desperados and he wouldn't have had any trouble in doing so by himself. Harris said he hadn't gotten a good look at the two and although he hadn't seen a horse he thought he'd seen a buggy nearby. When told of the reward he quickly left to pursue the two. All of these leads kept the Sheriff's Office quite busy.

As the search continued another story appeared in the paper that the jail break may have been prevented if Jailors had paid attention to inmate Ray Everett. Everett, who is confined at the jail awaiting Grand Jury action on a charge of arson for burning of the Cayuga village jail, was in the habit of sending out so many letters to friends and counsel, allegedly wrote of the escape plans and the fact that he'd been invited to participate.

Since Everett had written so many other letters of happenings at the jail that were investigated and found to be unfounded his letter of the jail break was considered another one of his "fabrications of an unoccupied mind." His letter had been set aside without further investigation.

On Friday morning George Pollard of Clark Street Rd., five miles west of the city, reported someone had broken into his barn and stolen a pair of lines and a bridle, leaving behind an older pair. The pair left behind was later identified by Frank Casler, of Fleming, as the pair taken with his stolen horse and buggy. Under Sheriff Drake immediately began a search of roads west of Auburn.

At 900pm that evening Stephen Donovan, of Venice, needed help. Since he didn't have a phone he drove to Frank Saxon's general store nearby. After explaining his situation to Saxton the two men set off looking for Deputy Walker. When they located the Deputy near Moravia, Donovan told him of a young man who came to his farm Wednesday afternoon and offered to work for room and board. Donovan told the Deputy the young man left his farm around 700pm and he believed he'd stolen some money. He stated, however, when the young man returned at 800pm he returned the missing money and went to bed. He said as soon as he knew the man was sleeping he left to get help. The three men immediately drove to Donovan's farm where Deputy Walker found James Blake in a bedroom asleep. The arrest was made at 1100pm and Blake was returned to the County Jail. He told Deputy Walker when he and Comfort reached Venice they split up. He stated that Comfort continued south with the horse and buggy, attempting to reach Elmira, while he walked through the woods and came upon Donovan's farm. Deputies swarmed the southern end of the County and Comfort was apprehended a short time later by Under Sheriff Drake three miles south of King Ferry.

On Monday morning September 8th., both escapees were arraigned on new charges of Escape and Grand Larceny. Both plead innocent and were once again confined to jail without bail to await action of the October Grand

Jury. The October Grand Jury returned True Bills against both Blake and Comfort.

On Tuesday November 1, 1912, Blake and Comfort appeared before Justice S. Nelson Sawyer and plead guilty. District Attorney Albert Clark noted Blake had served time at Elmira for chronic truancy and requested prisoner be sentenced to state prison. Blake's attorney F.A. Mohr strongly argued for leniency noting his client's young age and the fact that he supported his ailing mother in Detroit. Even Charles Kanaley stated he desired Blake receive leniency. Justice Sawyer sentenced Blake to a year and a half at the Elmira Reformatory.

District Attorney Clark requested Comfort be ruled a habitual criminal in that he'd served time at both Auburn and Elmira Prisons for horse theft. His attorney Charles A. Wright admitted that his client seem to have a mania for horse theft but he had always taken good care of the horse and had never sold or harmed one. Justice Sawyer sentenced Comfort to six years and eleven months for horse theft and seven years for the escape. The charges of stealing Frank Casler's horse and buggy were suspended. Comfort will serve his time at Auburn Prison.

The sentencing of the two escapees ended a front page newspaper story that sold a lot of papers. As the two men were taken to prison things at the jail soon changed. The old iron grate was taken out and the duct was filled in with concrete. A Jailor was also assigned to work the overnight shift.

As an interesting side note....Charles Kanaley, was a well known native of Weedsport. He, along with his brother James, had continued operating a grocery store in Weedsport established by their father in 1877. A graduate of Weedsport High School, in his youth he gained a wide reputation as a baseball player and had played left field on the renowned Watson team. He played one season with Cortland in the NY State League, and later rejected offers to play in the major leagues to continue his business career. He served as a director of the First National Bank of Weedsport and was involved in many community affairs.

In the early 1920s, he and his wife Florence (nee Shepherd) moved to Chicago where he organized and became president of the Hamilton State

Bank. Upon retirement he served as vice president and managing director of the Patrician apartments in Chicago where he resided at the time of his death Saturday April 10, 1954. After funeral services in Chicago he was buried in All Saints Cemetery, in Des Plaines, Illinois.

Although many inventors had tinkered with and manufactured automobiles prior to the early 1900s, automobiles were relatively a "new invention" that few people could afford. So, when someone bought an automobile it was big news. Twice in those early years, Kanaley made the papers when he purchased new vehicles. Early on, when he bought a Winton touring car and in 1910 when he purchased the 1910 Oakland runabout that was stolen by Blake at Lakeside Park. The car was described as a bright red two seater, with black striping, gas tank mounted on the back, zig-zag windshield and no top. Also attached to the vehicle were four new Springfield-Kelly 32" x 3 ½" tires. A snazzy ride for the times!

1910 Oakland two seat runabout similar to Charles Kanaley's with the exception of roof

Buggy similar to Frank Casler's

BANDIT'S ROBBERY GOES WRONG

Edward H. Bradt, of Syracuse and was an agent for the St. Paul Insurance Company. He came to Auburn Thursday morning February 23, 1922, for the purpose of collecting premiums. His day in Auburn would soon turn into a long and trying one.

Upon reaching Auburn, he engaged taxi driver John Muldoon to transport him to his many stops throughout the City. The day was going as planned when Muldoon told Bradt that he needed to make a stop. Around 1100am, near the corner of Genesee and North Streets, Muldoon stopped and met up with his friend John Stopyra, of 210 State Street. After a short discussion, Muldoon returned to the cab and he and Bradt continued on their way.

At approximately 730pm, as the two men drove up Elizabeth Street, a man stepped into the roadway and stopped the cab. When he approached Mr. Bradt he held a blue barreled .38 caliber revolver in his hand. He jammed the gun into Bradt's ribs and demanded all of Bradt's money. When Bradt somewhat hesitated, the bandit reached into Bradt's pocket, as if he knew where the bankroll was kept, and took it. He then turned his attention to Muldoon and took his fare money. The robbery was over in what seemed like an instant as the bandit jumped into a car and sped away. Muldoon turned his cab around and made his way to the Police station where he and Bradt reported the robbery. Bradt reported approximately $200.00 had been taken while Muldoon said he parted with $2.00. The coppers quickly got down to work.

For the rest of the evening and all day Friday Detective Sgt. Patrick Graney, along with Patrol Sgts. Dan Randall and Norman Parker and Officer Bill Brownhill checked several leads and their "sources." They then went looking to speak with Muldoon again only to find that he and his friend John Stopyra were out of town partying. As Saturday morning rolled around, Police finally located their quarry together at the Central Restaurant, on North Street. The duo's breakfast feast was interrupted when the quartet of coppers swooped in and invited them to Headquarters.

At the station, things didn't go well for the two men. Stopyra was in possession of a large unaccountable sum of money and Muldoon quickly cracked. He told Police that as he drove Bradt around town he had met up with Stopyra, who after seeing Bradt with a large bankroll suggested that they rob him. Muldoon confessed that at first he didn't want to go along with it but after discussing it with Stopyra he changed his mind. Muldoon continued…Stopyra would borrow a car and they would meet up later on Elizabeth Street to stage the robbery. Faced with Muldoon's confession, Stopyra soon changed his tune and told the coppers where they could find the weapon involved. Coppers not only found the .38 handgun under his mattress but also a "wicked little billy" next to it. Both items were reported to now be at Police Headquarters and out of commission for all time. Only a small portion of Bradt's money was recovered. It seems the partying duo had had quite a night out.

In March, Muldoon and Stopyra were both indicted for Robbery First Degree and various other charges associated with the crime. After both pled innocent, Muldoon posted a $1,500.00 bond to remain free. Stopyra, unable to come up with the required $2,000.00 bond was sent to County Jail.

On Monday morning June 5, 1922, both men appeared in County Court before Judge Edgar S. Mosher. Both pled guilty. Before sentencing the men, Judge Mosher asked them if there was anything they wished to say. Muldoon, with tears streaming from his eyes, told the Court that he had been intoxicated at the time and that some of the stuff that produced his intoxication had been provided by his passenger (Bradt). Stopyra chose not to say anything. Judge Mosher, after stressing the disgrace both men had brought upon their families, then stated that he himself had made an investigation of the crime and found that a practically concerted plan had been staged to hold up Bradt and their story as given to the Police was virtually a framed-up story. He went on to say that there was no one more willing than he to give a boy a chance, but by his investigation, he came to the conclusion that neither could be classed as first offenders, that both were principals in the robbery and should receive the same punishment. He then sentenced both men to serve two to four years in a State Prison facility.

After the sentencing, Police Chief William Bell, noted that there were too many people in the City acting as taxi operators. He again brought to the City Council's attention that a City ordinance was needed to deal with the licensing of chauffeur and taxi licenses to only those deemed favorable by the Police.

As for the two robbers, their night out would be their last for a long, long time.

MURDER IN CAYUGA

Some people said Asa Kline, of Cayuga and Luigi Rapito, of Auburn are the best of friends. But most agreed the two were bitter enemies when drinking and had threatened one another over what Asa perceived as Rapito's intimacy with his wife Harriet, and their 17 year old daughter Jennie.

Asa Kline was 49 years old and a village carpenter. He resided on Wheat Street in Cayuga, NY, with his wife Harriet, age 45, better known as Hattie, and their four children.

Luigi Rapito was 32 years old and was better known as Louie by most of his friends. He was employed at International Harvester plant No. 2 and resided at 17 Coon Street (now Venice St.), in Auburn. He came to America in 1909 or 1910 from Naples, Italy. After a short stay in New York City he came to Auburn and obtained work at the Columbian Rope Company. He had also worked at Dunn & McCarthy and at one point he ran a small lunch room opposite the Jefferson Theater on State Street. When WW 1 started in Europe, he returned to Italy and served in the Italian Army. He saw action on the front lines in Austria and France, and was wounded twice, once in the hip and once in the arm. In 1919 he was honorable discharged and married soon thereafter. He returned to the US in 1920 leaving behind his wife and one small child. Upon his return he went to work for Ralph Salata as a section hand for the NY Central Railroad at Cayuga. While working in Cayuga, he boarded with Joseph DiLorenzo in that village. He later returned to Auburn where he was working at IH and residing on Coon Street up until the evening of Sunday March 23, 1924.

On Sunday afternoon March 23, 1924, Joseph DiLorenzo, of Cayuga (in many newspaper accounts the name was spelled Lorenzo) was visiting friends in Auburn when he ran into Louie on Orchard Street where several men were drinking and playing an Italian game of Morra (Fingers). As Louie and Joe had a few drinks, Louie told Joe that he had received a registered letter from Hattie Kline inviting him to visit the family and he was planning on catching the afternoon train to Cayuga to do so. Since it was getting late, Joe agreed to accompany him and the two men caught the 6:22pm train to Cayuga.

Upon reaching Cayuga, Joe headed home, just a short distance from the depot, and Louie headed to the Kline residence. Upon reaching Kline's, he found the family at home and George Annin, of Cayuga visiting with Asa. Louie spoke with Hattie for a short time and said he'd return a little later. He left and went to DiLorenzo's where he and Joe had a drink while Joe's wife Michaelana prepared supper. A short time later Asa Kline arrived at DiLorenzo's and he wasn't in a good mood. He told Louie to stop bothering his family, particularly his wife and daughter Jennie, or there would be trouble. The two men began to argue....Louie denied he had bothered the two women and told Asa to shut up. As the two men continued arguing DiLorenzo begged them not to cause trouble in his home as his family was present. His plea fell on deaf ears as the argument intensified. When Louie went to leave Asa stopped him and Louie pushed him aside and told him to "keep still or I'll get you," to which Asa replied "why, what do you want to kill me?" With that Asa turned and started for the door but Louie grabbed him by the shoulder with his left hand, swung him around and struck him in the face with a stiletto he was holding in his right hand. The stiletto entered Asa's left eye and punctured the lining of his brain. Asa raised his hands to his face and while covering his eye yelled "Louie what have you done?" With that Louie made a quick exit out the back door while Asa stumbled out the front door and headed home, leaving a trail of blood along his route.

ASA CLINE, STABBED IN EYE BY AN ITALIAN, IS EXPECTED TO LIVE

All Night Search Fails to Locate Assailant of Cayuga Carpenter—Stiletto Blade Punctures Brain Covering.

Citizen headline Monday 3/24/1924

Doctor J.H. Wilbeck, of Cayuga, was summoned to the Kline home as was Cayuga Constable George Marsh. Dr. Wilbeck treated Asa's wound and ordered that he immediately be taken to the hospital in Auburn. Arrangements were made to transport Kline in a car to the hospital accompanied by Constable Marsh. Upon reaching Auburn City Hospital doctors quickly determined surgery was necessary and Asa was rushed into the OR. Doctor Jason L. Wiley, an eye specialist, assisted by Doctors R.C. Almy and A.J. Bennett, performed the operation to remove Asa's left eye. District Attorney Benn Kenyon and Sheriff Edwin Mosher waited in the recovery room but Asa wasn't in any condition to provide much information as to who had stabbed him or why. The Sheriff left for Cayuga and DiLorenzo's house.

In Cayuga, the Sheriff and his deputies immediately went to DiLeorenzo's home and quickly learned that it was Luigi Rapito that had stabbed Kline. DiLorenzo then handed over a three inch stiletto he claimed he'd found under a table after the incident. He stated the weapon belonged to Rapito. During a search of the room where the incident occurred an ice pick was found in a cabinet drawer. Both the stiletto and ice pick were seized by the Sheriff as evidence.

After a search of the village the Sheriff and his men returned to Auburn. Believing that Rapito had returned to his Coon Street home the Auburn Police Department was notified. Auburn Police Captain Edward Holmes assigned Sergeant Daniel Randall and Officer Paul Tata to assist the Sheriff's men. The two Coppers along with the Sheriff went to Rapito's Coon Street home all to no avail. During a quick search of his premises 21 letters from Hattie Kline to Rapito were found in a trunk. They were taken as possible evidence. The search for Rapito continued throughout the night. Police and Sheriff's Deputies spoke with several residents and friends of Rapito's in the city's Italian colony while roadblocks were setup on all roads leading out of the city. The Sheriff made sure wanted posters were distributed describing Rapito as an Italian male, age 32, 5'4", 145 pounds, black hair, dark complexion, smooth face and flat nose, good teeth, walks erect, occupation laborer.

As the search for Rapito continued, at 6:00am Wednesday morning March 26th., Kline died while still confined at the hospital. Reports from the hospital indicate Kline had been very restless all night and shortly before his death he became so violent that orderlies had to subdue him. Hospital authorities were of the opinion that if he didn't recover he would go insane.

Kline's death intensified the search for Rapito as the Sheriff's men followed leads that took them to Seneca Falls, Waterloo and Rochester.

MURDER CHARGE
LUIGI RAPOTI IS NOW OBJECT OF MAN HUNT

Clues to His Whereabouts Are Lacking But Strong Chain of Evidence Is Welded, Linking Him to Brawl in Lorenzo Home.

Citizen headline Wed. 3/26/24

Finally, early on Friday morning March 28th., Sheriff Mosher, Under Sheriff Charles Dayton and Deputy Stephen Bissi drove out to the farm of Mike Colfrencesco, in Throop. While Sheriff Mosher guarded the perimeter of the home, Under Sheriff Dayton and Deputy Bissi knocked on the door and were greeted by Colfrencesco's wife Serafino. They informed her that they were there to look for Luigi Rapito. At first she hesitated, but then told the men that they could find him upstairs. The two deputies cautiously made their way upstairs and quickly located Rapito hiding under a pile of clothes in one of the bedrooms.

Now under arrest for Murder First Degree he was brought to District Attorney Benn Kenyon's office. Court interpreter Tony Orapello was called in to take Rapito's statement. Rapito remained calm as the questioning, all spoken in Italian by Orapello, began. Rapito admitted he and Kline had been arguing and that he had struck Kline but denied he killed him. He told investigators he had been intoxicated and only went into hiding after learning he had been accused of the murder. He was taken before Justice Louis K.R. Laird for arraignment on the charge of Murder in the First Degree. He pled not guilty and was quickly sent to County Jail without bail to await further action by the May Grand Jury. On April 23rd., Joe DiLorenzo, Hattie and Jennie Kline were taken into custody and held as material witnesses.

The Grand Jury indicted Rapito for the murder. A trial date was set for early September before Supreme Court Justice Adelbert P. Rich. Rapito will be defended by Auburn attorneys Frank S. Coburn and Richard T. Anderson. DA Benn Kenyon, assisted by ADA James J. Hosmer will prosecute. The murder trial will be the first case heard in the newly repaired Court House since the fire in April 1922.

The trial began on Monday September 8, 1924. After a day and a half of jury selection the court room was jammed with spectators when DA Kenyon made his opening remarks telling jurors that the prosecution would prove beyond any reasonable doubt Rapito intentionally killed Kline as the two men argued over Rapito's attention towards Kline's wife and 17 year old daughter. Defense attorney Frank Coburn followed by telling jurors it wasn't Rapito that killed Kline but Joseph DiLorenzo, who at one time had pursued

Mrs. Kline and wanted her to elope with him. Kline's three brothers Amos and William, both of Seneca Falls, and Burt of Rochester were all present in the court room.

DA Kenyon began his prosecution by calling George Annin, Dr. Witbeck and Constable George Marsh to the stand. Next up were Sheriff Mosher, Under Sheriff Dayton and Deputy Bissi. They testified to the search of DiLorenzo's home after the incident and to the seizure of the stiletto and ice pick, the letters found at Rapito's home and to finding Raptio at Colfrencesco's home in Throop. The stiletto and ice pick were placed into evidence. Benny Marsh, of 110 ½ Clark Street and Albert Madero, of Cottage Street both testified how Rapito came to Marsh's home the night of the assault and told them he'd had trouble in Cayuga. Emil J.Kramer testified he had been called to DiLornezo's home on the night of the assault to photograph the scene. He identified the pictures he'd taken that were then placed into evidence.

Tony Manciano, of 7 Coon Street, was then called to the stand. He stated Rapito had boarded at his home for some time before the Cayuga incident. That on the morning after the stabbing Rapito came home and told him that he'd had trouble in Cayuga and had stabbed Asa Kline in the face. Manciano said Rapito asked for some money but when it wasn't forthcoming he went away and never returned. Under cross examination he stated that he was a brother-in-law to Joseph DiLorenzo. When defense attorney Coburn asked "Did you understand that Rapito or DiLorenzo killed Kline," DA Kenyon objected and was sustained by Judge Rich.

Tony Testa of Chestnut Street testified about two years ago, while employed by the New York Central in Cayuga, he worked with Rapito. He stated at that time he had turned a grindstone for Rapito to make a three cornered knife and also a flat knife, both from file. He could not say that the stiletto in evidence was the same one only that it looked like it.

Mike Colfrencesco and his wife Serafino were next to testify. Mr. Colfrencesco testified to Rapito coming to his home the morning after the Cayuga incident and asking him if he could stay for a couple of days due to trouble he'd had in Auburn. Colfrencesco stated he told Rapito he could stay and help out on the farm by cutting wood. He told jurors Rapito never did any work, "he got up around ten in the morning and said he wasn't feeling well." Mrs. Colfrencesco confirmed same, stating that "when Louie got up he said he didn't feel well. I fed him breakfast and told him to watch the kids while I did my chores." She stated he was very good with the children. She then told jurors of the morning the Sheriff's men came to their home, "When Louie saw the car approaching he said "they're here for me, you tell them I'm not here, you haven't seen me," he then went upstairs where the Sheriff's men found him." She identified Rapito as the man at her house.

The court room was full the day Joe Dilorenzo was called to testify. DiLorenzo recounted his meeting up with Rapito in Auburn the day of the assault and the events leading up to the fight between Rapito and Kline at his home. He told the jurors Kline accused Rapito of harassing his wife and daughter and warned him to stay away from his family. He recalled how Rapito had told him that he (Rapito) could do anything he wanted to with Mrs. Kline and Jennie, anytime that he wanted to. He said Rapito had told him one time Asa had caught him in bed with Jennie and he was very angry.

Dilorenzo stated Rapito had frequently spent the night at Kline's while Asa was working in Rochester. He recounted the argument and fight the two men had and of witnessing Rapito strike Kline in the eye with the stiletto. He stated he hadn't read the letter from Mrs. Kline inviting Rapito to visit, that Rapito had only shown it to him. He said he found the stiletto under a table after Rapito had used it and left his home. He stated Rapito came back about fifteen minutes later and said he was going to Rochester....at this statement Rapito snickered audibly. On cross examination defense attorney Coburn went right after DiLorenzo. Questioning him about his pursuit of Hattie Kline, ownership of the stiletto—accusing him of owning it, his use of it to threaten his wife Michaelana and at one point his use of it to stab her during an argument, and his motive for killing Kline. DiLorenzo denied everything Coburn threw at him. He was somewhat rattled when he left the stand.

Joe's wife Michaelana was next to testify. She stated she hadn't witnessed the stabbing but confirmed most of what her husband had testified to regarding the argument between the two men. DiLorenzo's son Joseph was then called and testified that they were eating supper when Kline and Rapito began arguing. The young good looking boy stated that during the argument Rapito pulled a stiletto from his pocket, reached up and stabbed Kline in the eye. The boy stood up and dramatically demonstrated how the stiletto was drawn and the blow struck.

When Hattie Kline entered the court room she was dressed entirely in black. She only glanced at Raptio once and never looked at him again or acknowledged him. She testified she had met Rapito two years ago in Cayuga while he was working for the railroad and boarding at DiLorenzo's. She stated Rapito had visited with her family many times and was always a gentleman. She told how her husband often accused her and their daughter Jennie of being intimate with several different men. She said "it was like a hobby of his to accuse us of being intimate with men, but more so with Louie." She denied she or Jennie had ever had such a relationship. She recalled one time when Rapito was visiting the family her husband had come from upstairs entered the room she and Rapito were in, "he called Louie a vile name, accused him of being intimate with me and struck Louie in the back of the head with a board." She said "Louie swore and told Asa "I don't want your wife, I'll get you for that." She said she saw Rapito later that night pacing back and forth across the street from their home. She identified all but two of the 21 letters she'd written to Rapito. At that point defense attorney Coburn objected to the letters being placed into evidence and Judge Rich ruled in his favor, noting that it could not be shown Rapito ever responded to them or that Asa Kline had ever known about them.

Under cross examination she continued to deny she had any intimate relationship with Rapito. She admitted she had sent a registered letter to Rapito days before the stabbing requesting he come over to Cayuga to visit. She then said there was no time set and the invitation was to see all the family. When asked by defense attorney Coburn if Rapito had any occasion to spend the night at her home when her husband was out of town she replied yes. She went on to explain when her husband took a job in Rochester for three months he would come home once a month, usually on a weekend, to visit. She stated it was during this three month period, while her husband was in Rochester, that Rapito had spent 6 or 7 nights at her home. When Coburn pressed his questioning on her husband's accusing her and their daughter of being intimate with Rapito she replied "He was always talking about intimacies. He thought a lot of things, but there is a lot of difference between what you think and what you know." When asked if Rapito had ever asked her to elope she replied "No. I'm pretty old to elope. I would have done that years ago if I wanted to." When she then laughed at her assertion Justice Rich had to rap for order and silence because of all the tittering about the court room. Coburn continued his questioning, asking her if she'd been intimate with Joe Dilorenzo. She denied she'd ever been intimate with DiLorenzo or any other man. When Coburn questioned if DiLorenzo had ever asked her to run off with him she replied yes. She stated she had gone to Seneca Falls to visit her mother and watch the fireworks and had seen DiLorenzo there. At that time he asked her to run away with him but she told him "I have four wonderful children, why would I run away with you?" She stated she spent the night in Seneca Falls and stayed at her mother's home. All during Mrs. Kline's testimony Raptio sat nervously at the defense table and the smile that was usually on his face had disappeared.

Jennie Kline, age 17, a small and not bad looking girl was called next to testify. In the hour she was on the stand she admitted she had had illicit intercourse with Rapito. She stated the intimate relationship began about two years ago. She told how her father had once caught them and threatened to have her arrested on that account. She also acknowledged Rapito had spent nights at their home while her father was out of town. When several observers in the court room snickered at some of her answers Justice Rich directed two rows of benches in one section of the room be cleared where the tittering and noise was apparently the loudest. He then made it clear that the trial of a man for his life was a serious matter and that mirth and noise would not be permitted. She was questioned about her time in jail and about passing notes out of a jail window (accusations were made she was attempting to communicate with Rapito) but she denied she'd ever passed a note out of the jail. During a recess Jennie was attended to by her uncles. She stated that her conscience compelled her to tell the truth and that it was the right thing to do.

Tilts between DA Kenyon and defense attorney Coburn became so bad that Judge Rich rapped for silence reminding the two attorneys "We are all getting nervous." Doctor Wiley, the OR doctor that removed Kline's eye was then called to testify. He stated that the operation was necessary to save Kline's life. He further stated that the blood clot found pressing on the brain was more the cause of death than meningitis and the cause of the blood clot was the stabbing. Coburn's cross examination of the Doctor was directed at the meningitis and blood clot as causes for Kline's death noting that Kline had lived for three days after the stabbing incident.

Coroner Paul M. Parker, of Moravia, was the last witness to be called for the prosecution. He testified as to performing the autopsy noting that Kline's left eye had been removed at the time. He described the wound in said eye socket and also the fracture of the bone structure behind the eye socket. He stated the wound was downward and inward for 3 ¾ inches into the eye socket and punctured the lining of the brain. A section of Kline's skull was displayed for the jurors to see just how the wound entered the eye socket. Once again Coburn's cross examination concerned the blood clot and meningitis. It was clear he was attempting to persuade jurors the cause of Kline's death, three days after the incident, was either the meningitis or the blood clot.

The defense then went to work. Called to the stand the first set of witnesses were more or less character witnesses. Cayuga residents Romaine Candee (a former 30 year justice of the peace), R.T. Durlong (village merchant & barber) and Mrs. Mersereau (40 year village resident), then former work associates James Quill, Supervisor of the Auburn Water Department and Frank F. Bohn, a foreman at International Harvester. All testified to knowing Rapito and spoke of his good character, ethics and job performance. The court room was full the days Albert H. Hamilton, Auburn criminologist, and Doctor C.F. McCarthy were called to the stand.

In 1908, after years of owning a successful Auburn drug store, Alert Hamilton began promoting himself as a criminologist. After being called to the stand he stated he had testified in 178 homicide cases in which stilettos, knives, daggers and razors had been used. He testified that he had examined the ice pick and stiletto involved with the case under a microscope. He stated the end of the ice pick was blunted and roughened. That one and a half inches from the point there was dried syrup of some type which he could not give the origin. He also noted that on the point was a human hair about 3/8" long, one end of which was fastened to the point and the other end free. He continued that he was unable to determine whether the hair was from an eyebrow or eyewinker. Mr. Hamilton set up the microscope so that Judge Rich, the jurors, the attorneys and physicians in the court room could see it. Doctor H.L. Davenport examined the hair through the microscope as he will be called as a rebuttal witness. Hamilton stated there was nothing about the ice pick to indicate it had been made from a file.

He went on to say his examination of the stiletto found no blood stains on it. Further that it is physically impossible for a metallic instrument to pass through the eye socket to the bony structure of the skull and be withdrawn without having blood on it.

Hamilton also testified that he had examined the section of Kline's skull that was in evidence. He stated that it would have been impossible for a three cornered stiletto to have made a round hole as indicated unless the stiletto had been used as a reamer. Further from his examination he stated that there was no indication of the weapon being used for any such purpose.

The next witness for the defense was Doctor C.F. McCarthy, physician and surgeon for 34 years. He testified that the operation for the removal of the left eye is quite apt to be followed by meningitis and in his opinion Kline's operation for the removal of his eye was not necessary to save his life or the sight of his other eye. He also stated there was danger of infection from probing of the wound. He contended that the clot of blood described as being found in Kline's brain would have been followed by death or the patient would have shown signs of paralysis. He stated the blood clot was not at the base of Kline's brain at the time of his death. He was given a thorough cross examination by DA Kenyon.

Finally the time came everyone was waiting for.... the crowded court room would hear from "the lonely immigrant boy" Lugi "Louie" Rapito took the stand. Court interpreter Tony Orapello was put to use as some of the questions and answers were spoken in Italian. Defense attorney Anderson's questioning began slowly as he had Rapito recount his upbringing in Italy, coming to the States and eventually to Auburn, how he returned to Italy to serve in the Italian Army during WW 1 and that he married after the war and had a wife and small child in Italy. Rapito went on to tell the jurors how eventually he returned to Auburn and meeting DiLorenzo and Kline while working in Cayuga. He stated he and Asa were good friends, that they often visited one another and on a couple of occasions Asa had even stayed overnight at his place. He denied he had pursued or ever had a relationship with either Hattie or Jennie Kline, or that Asa had ever accused him of that or struck him with a board. He also denied he had ever threatened to harm Asa. A gasp was heard in the court room was when defense attorney Anderson asked for the stiletto and then handed it to Rapito. When asked if it belonged to him Rapito replied "No. The only time I ever saw it was at DiLorenzo's home." He went on to say DiLorenzo had it grinded at the rail crew house. He then recounted how twice he had to take it away from DiLorenzo when he was arguing with his wife and threatened her with it. He denied he ever owned a stiletto or ever carried one. Rapito went on to say the night of the incident he wasn't feeling well and was lying on DiLorenzo's couch when Kline came over. He said that DiLorenzo and Kline got into a heated argument and "I went outside. When I came back in Asa was bleeding and Joe told me that I should get out of there."

Under an intense cross examination by DA Kenyon, Rapito denied he stabbed Kline or ever owned or carried the stiletto involved in the case. He said the first time he ever saw the weapon was when DiLorenzo was grinding it down from a three point file in the railroad tool house in Cayuga. He denied he had intimate relationships with Hattie and Jennie Kline. He stated that Asa had never accused him of that and had never caught him and Jennie in bed. He denied Asa had ever struck him with a board or that he threatened to get Kline. He contended emphatically that he was a pal of Kline. He did admit that he never told Kline on the night of the incident that DiLorenzo had accused Kline of saying he (Rapito) had been intimate with Kline's wife. When asked about discrepancies in his statement taken on the day of his arrest, particularity that he and Kline were arguing and he had struck Kline several times, and his present testimony he stated he couldn't remember a lot of the details and then denied he signed the statement. DA Kenyon then brought out the fact that "several witnesses were present during the questioning and taking of the statement which you gave willingly and did not seem nervous or excited," but Rapito continued to deny he had signed the statement. Rapito said on the night of the stabbing affray it was Joe and Asa that were arguing and that it was Joe that scared him away from the scene. He stated "I only tried to stay out of the way after seeing in the paper I was being accused of murder. So I went to Colfrencesco's farm because I knew him." DA Kenyon was unable to shake Rapito who stuck to his story.

On Thursday September 18th., after several rebuttal witnesses were called by both the prosecution and defense teams, DA Kenyon and defense attorney Coburn made their summations. At 3:45pm the jury began their deliberations. At 8:45pm the jury announced they had reached their verdict. By 9:20pm the Judge, attorneys and the defendant were all collected in the court room as the jury announced they had found Rapito guilty of Murder in the First Degree. Defense attorneys Coburn and Anderson attempted to have the verdict thrown out for lack of evidence but were over ruled. Their attempt to have sentencing postponed was withdrawn when they could show no reason to do so and Judge Rich announced he was ready to sentence

the defendant. The Judge then sentenced Rapito to be taken to Sing Sing Prison within ten days to be executed the week of November 2nd.. Rapito was pale and trembling as he was escorted back to the County Jail. DA Kenyon then moved that Hattie & Jennie Kline be released from County Jail, where they have been held as material witnesses since April 23rd., same was ordered by Judge Rich. It is noted that each women was paid $25.00 for their time spent in lock up.

Under tight security and secrecy, late Saturday night September 20th., Rapito was escorted to Sing Sing Prison by Sheriff Mosher, Under Sheriff Dayton and Sing Sing guard Robert Smith, returning from a vacation in Auburn. A second Sheriff's vehicle with Deputies Jack Callahan and Jerry Murray with a State Trooper from the Port Byron station followed close behind. Near Syracuse a State Police unit with two husky Troopers joined the protection squad. Their arrival at the New York Central station in Syracuse caused a little stir but not enough to excite anyone. Rapito, who has refused to shave since his conviction was heard telling his escorts "It's awful to think those two fellows out in Chicago got away with a life sentence after admitting killing that kid (reference to Nathan Leopold & Richard Loeb/murder of 14 yr. old 5/21/24) and I am sentenced to the chair when I didn't do anything." Rapito stated that the first thing he planned to do upon reaching Sing Sing was contact a Catholic priest. He said he had confidence that his attorneys would win an appeal and save him from the death chamber. Before boarding the train Rapito said goodbyes to the Deputies and Troopers who accompanied him to Syracuse. The next morning Sheriff Mosher sent a telegram declaring Rapito had been delivered to Sing Sing without incident and he and Under Sheriff Dayton were en-route home.

Over the next two years Rapito's execution was postponed twice as his appeals worked their way through the court system. When attorneys Coburn and Anderson failed to win a new trial or a life sentence a new execution date was set for Thursday January 28, 1926. The two attorneys worked feverishly appealing to Governor Smith for executive clemency. The Governor ordered a special panel to review the trial, evidence and proceedings and stated he would make his decision after a thorough review of the panel's findings.

On Thursday January 28th., all of Coburn's and Anderson's last minute calls to Sing Sing confirmed their darkest fears….Rapito had been executed at 11:05pm. It was reported Rapito had spent the day nervously in his cell and had his last meal of steak and mushrooms, bread, butter and cocoanut pie with coffee at 500pm. At 1100pm he was taken from his cell and walked silently to the execution chamber between two guards and a Catholic priest.

He said nothing and left no last minute statement, by 1110pm his life was over. He was the first of two men executed that night.

Members of Auburn's Italian colony were surprised to hear Governor Smith had not granted clemency and a collection was taken up to have his body brought back to Auburn and buried. His body was brought back to Auburn via train on Saturday September 30th., and was taken to the undertaking parlors of William H. Meagher, on State Street. On Monday February 1st., services were held at Saint Francis d'Assissi Church, on Clark Street, with the Rev. D.E. Masselli officiating. Burial was at Saint Joseph's Cemetery, Fleming.

As an interesting side note....On Friday October 2, 1924, county inmate Francis O'Brien was transferred to Auburn Prison. During his search at the prison two saw blades were found in his shoes. The sheriff's office was immediately notified. After a brief investigation Sheriff Mosher reports he believes the two saw blades were smuggled into the jail for Lugi Rapito whose cell was next to O'Brien's. He stated investigators believe Rapito was going to use the saw blades to break out of the jail if he was found guilty. Since he was guarded day and night by two jailors he never had the chance to use them. They believe the blades were passed to O'Brien who was being transferred out of the jail in an attempt to conceal them. Sheriff Mosher stated O'Brien, who is dieing of turberculosis, would not give up any information regarding the two blades. O'Brien who has spent most of his life in jails and prisons was an officer of the Prison Welfare League, when he and Ambrose Geary escaped from Auburn Prison on Friday June 11, 1920. Both were apprehended a few months later in Troy. Geary is now on Sing Sing's death row for the murder of a drug store proprietor in Buffalo.

The second man executed with Rapito was Emil "Dutch" Klatt, a New Jersey gangster. Found guilty of Murder in the First Degree he had been on the run for nine years before being arrested for killing a policeman in Minneapolis. He along with co-conspirators William "Black Mack" McNamara, another NJ gangster, Kitty "Hoboken Kitty" McCormick, Antoinette George and Mary Siglio were all found guilty of murdering Georgorio George on Saturday January 15, 1916. It seems when Mrs. George fell in love with a young roomer she and her husband's sister Mary hired "Kitty" to have her husband killed. "Kitty" in turn hired Klatt and McNamara to do the job promising them $250.00 each after the insurance money was paid. Klatt and McNamara were sentenced to death, the three females were sentenced to serve 20 years to life. In 1925 McNamara was given a life sentence for his testimony at Klatt's trial. In 1930 McNamara and

McCormick were paroled along with Mrs. George. Mary Siglio died in prison. Klatt's last words were to curse McNamara for betraying him. All of them had spent time in Auburn Prison.

Services for Asa Kline were held on Friday March 28, 1924 at Sanderson's Undertaking Parlors, in Seneca Falls. He was buried in Springbrook Cemetery. Surviving are his wife, two daughters Jennie and Mrs. Helen Getter, two sons Charles and Carlton, his mother Mrs. Mary H. Kline, of Rochester, five brothers and two sisters.

MYSTERIOUS BLAST BLOWS LOCAL HOME APART

On Sunday February 12, 1933, the company clock at the E.D. Clapp Company, located at the corner of Genesee and Columbus Streets, had just struck 11:30pm as night watchman Fritz Kruger finished his rounds. There was a full moon shining down on the cold quiet street as Kruger struck up a conversation with William Taylor, an attendant at the Weeks Gasoline Station, located just across the corner from the Clapp Company. As the two men stood chatting they were jarred from their positions by a terrific blast and large sheets of fire that shot across Genesee Street and licked at the Genesee Street exterior wall of the Clapp shop.

The blast momentarily stunned the two men. Quickly regaining their senses they realized a house located a short distance away on Genesee Street had just exploded. While Taylor dashed to pull fire alarm box 41 located at the Clapp Company, Kruger ran to the nearest phone to notify the Fire Department.

The powerful explosion was sudden and it blew apart the home and businesses located at 294 Genesee Street. It sides were blown into the adjacent buildings on either side of it. The front of the building was entirely gone; its front door and windows had been blown across Genesee Street and hurled into the exterior wall of the Clapp Company. The roof had collapsed into the burning inferno providing it with more fodder to feed on. Large sheets of flame raced across Genesee Street and licked at the exterior wall of the Clapp shop where a 100 windows were broken by the blast and debris blown across the street.

As the Auburn Fire Department rolled west down Genesee Street hill the men could clearly see they weren't responding to a false alarm. From that distance they could see that a large fire was brewing and they knew they were in for a long night. As the trucks pulled up in front of 294 Genesee Street they found the building totally engulfed. The fire also began to burn the buildings on both sides of it. Fire Chief Fred J. Washburn knew that if the neighboring buildings became engulfed the whole block might go up in flames. As he directed his men fighting the fire a large effort was put into saving the adjacent buildings. The intense fire spewed embers into the sky creating a danger that the roofs on other nearby buildings and homes would catch fire. As homeowners kept a watchful eye on their homes, the roof and cupola at the Clapp Company caught fire twice but firemen and company employees quickly extinguished the danger.

The firefighters fought valiantly hoping to rescue anyone trapped inside the blazing inferno but soon realized it was a helpless situation, that anyone caught inside the burning home would have surely been killed in the blast and ensuing fire. When pieces of charred bone and flesh were found it was feared members of the Scro family had perished. Everyone was relieved when the bones and flesh were found to be pieces of meat blown out of the Baldessaro Meat Market.

294 Genesee Street, better known as the Scro Block, is owned by Salvadore "Sam" Scro. He occupies the upper apartment with his wife Mary and three children. In the lower street level portion of the building he conducted a wholesale grocery which was known for its imported olive oil and cheese emporium. Baldessaro Meat Market also occupied a lower level store front in the same building. The whereabouts of the Scro family was unknown and many feared they had been caught inside the burning home.

The large tenement house at 296 Genesee Street, owned by Augustino Santino, is occupied by Robert Cunningham, his two young sons Kenneth and Bob and his mother Mrs. Jeannie Walker. Mr. Cunningham stated the blast shook his home and jarred him from his bed. He said within seconds of the blast a large piece of flaming material was blown through his bedroom window setting the bedding on fire. They barely had time to escape the dwelling and fled the burning structure bare footed and clad only in their night clothes. Jerry Madden, who occupies an apartment in the same building was rendered ill from smoke inhalation and exposure and was taken to City Hospital by Prowl Car Officer Charles Wenner. He was treated by Doctor C.H. Maxwell and ordered to spend the night for observation.

The double house at 292 Genesee Street, owned by Alphonso Passarello, is occupied by James Parks and his family. Awaken by the blast they too escaped only in their night clothes. Both families took shelter at Weeks Gasoline station where they were treated for cuts to their feet and exposure. Both families were later taken in by family members and friends and made comfortable for the rest of the night.

At 290 ½ Genesee Street, barber Charles Passerello said he was just going to bed when the whole building shook and knocked his bed across the room. He stated he was spun around and felt as if he'd been struck a heavy blow. He then saw flames shooting out from the building next door. Mr. Passerello said he managed to grab some belongings and quickly ran out of the building.

In the same house were Alphonso Passerello, his wife, their two year old daughter and four month old infant. He told a reporter that he was awoken when he heard something large slam into the side of his home. He stated the noise woke his family and within a few seconds something crashed through the bedroom window. He grabbed his children and pushed his wife out of the bedroom and rushed his family out into the street. The loud blast shook homes in the immediate area and awoke residents several blocks away. Debris was thrown a distance of a two blocks in every direction and the paint on several cars parked close to the intense blast and fire had been scorched. Within ten minutes a crowd had gathered and the Auburn Police closed Genesee Street and set up barricades for crowd control. As all this was occurring Sam Scro and his family arrived at the scene. Sam Scro was shocked at what he saw; the fire had destroyed his whole business and living quarters. He told Fire Chief Washburn that he had no idea what would have caused the fire, that there wasn't anything in the basement that would have caused an explosion. He stated that he and his family had left home around

4:00pm to visit relatives on Wright Avenue. He said he and his children remained at his brother's home while his wife and sister-in-law went uptown to catch a show. It was a lucky day for the family for if they'd been at home when the explosion occurred they probably would all have been killed.

As the firemen fought the blaze the frigid temperature turned them into walking icicles. Linemen from the Empire Power and Electric Company were kept busy cutting power lines in the immediate vicinity to prevent firemen or pedestrians from accidentally coming into contact with fallen live lines. Other power and electric company crews were kept busy when three hundred homes in the area went without gas after a broken gas line flooded with water. The street was turning into an ice rink.

The explosion Sunday Feb. 12, 1933 at 294 Genesee St., totally destroyed Scro grocery & Baldessaro Meat Market and heavily damaged nearby buildings.

After battling the stubborn blaze for close to two hours the firemen finally brought the situation under control. The Scro home was totally destroyed and the two buildings on either side of it were heavily damaged. At what was left of the Parks' home, firefighters found the family's small terrier dog and two canary birds had somehow survived. The pets were returned to the family. The residents were advised they would not be allowed to enter the site until it had been made safe to do so.

ALONG THESE STREETS AND ROADS

As the men continued their clean up operations Chief Wasburn stated an investigation as to what caused the explosion and fire would begin as soon as he was assured all hot spots had been extinguished and the structural security of the buildings was checked to ensure the safety of the men before they entered the ravaged site. Auburn Police Chief Chester Bills assigned Detective William Graney to assist the Fire Department and City Building Inspector David J. Nolin with the investigation.

Another view of the damage to 294 Genesee St.

Rumors were wild and many thought a "pineapple bomb" had been tossed into Scro's grocery. Others believed it was a gas leak that caused the large destructive explosion. It took another whole day to pump the water out of the basements and ensure the structure was safe enough for the men to enter the site. At one point a small flare up occurred but was quickly extinguished by firemen left at the scene. City Street Superintendent Merritt E. Tice directed a crew and machinery removing debris from the site so investigators could reach the basement. A large effort is being made to get into the basement to check the gas line connections. As the clean up continued, Fire Captain H. Clyde Beacham, of Hose Company 1, fell through a hole in the floor. He had been walking across the remnants when he stepped on some weakened boards and went almost out of sight. He wasn't injured and continued his duties.

All property owners and their tenants were interviewed and their statements were taken by investigators. Sam Scro was interviewed by District Attorney Erwin Blauvelt and Police Chief Bills. He denied he had any enemies that would burn out his business and or attempt to kill him and his family. He denied he had recently installed a new heating system and said he had been using the same boiler and steam heating plant that has been in place for a number of years. He also noted that there was an auxiliary hot water heating system in the basement not in use. He stated he had no idea how the fire started and that nothing was stored in the basement or near the heating unit that would have caused an explosion.

Fire Chief Washburn stated the fire started in northwest corner of the basement. He doesn't believe any type of explosive device was used or thrown into the building. The buildings front door which had been blown across Genesee Street and found thrown against the exterior wall of the Clapp shop is in Police custody as they check it for pry marks and look over its locking device. When investigators were finally able to get into the basement the heating units, gas meters and lines were all checked and found to be intact. It took several months before officials released a report which stated although no conclusive cause was determined it was their belief the explosion was the result of gas leak. That gas fumes were ignited when they came into contact with the heating unit.

In April 1933, Sam Scro's wife Mary along with The Home, Fire & Marine Insurance Company and The American Insurance Company filed suit against Empire Power and Electric Company. In paperwork filed with the court the Scros report the mortgage on their property is $15,000.00; the building including their grocery store and living quarters and its contents were insured for $25,000.00. Mrs. Scro hopes to recover approximately $9,300.00 in damages to the building and personal property lost in the explosion and fire. The two insurance companies are seeking to recover approximately $15,200.00 they paid out as a result of the incident. The Scros and insurance companies were represented by the Syracuse law firm of Searl & McElroy; the Auburn law firm of Noble, Leary & Leary represented the power company.

Attorneys on both sides filed motions that delayed the trial and getting postponed to the next session of Supreme Court. The case was finally scheduled to be heard in May 1936 in front of Justice John C. Wheeler. Several witnesses were called by the plaintiffs including Fritz Kruger, William Taylor, Sam Scro, Agosto Santino, John B. Alger, Robert Cunningham, John Madden and experts Albert H. Hamilton, of Auburn and F. Austin Clymer, of Syracuse and formerly of Auburn.

Much ado was given when an old rusty hot water heater, a relic collected from the debris of the former Scro block, was brought into the court room. Hamilton testified he had examined the heater and found it to be defective and the cause of the fire and explosion. His testimony was detailed in chemical and microscopic examinations he made after the fire. He stated that the fire started before the explosion from escaping gas from the main large distributor pipe in the basement of the automatic gas heater at a time when the water heater pilot light was out. He was on the witness stand for several hours and his cross examination was quite intense. The plaintiff's attorneys rested after Hamilton's final testimony. At that point the defendant's attorney Percy E. Leary argued for a non-suit and dismissal of the complaint. He characterized the testimony and theory of the plaintiff's case as speculative from A to Z with little direct evidence as to the cause of the fire and explosion. Attorney Clifford H. Searl, for the plaintiffs opposed. Justice Wheeler denied the motion stating that there was a question of fact for the jury to pass on.

Leary then called Louis Schnidman to the stand. Mr. Schnidman is employed as a research director by the Rochester Gas & Electric Company, and connected with the research department of the American Gas Association. His testimony completely combated the plaintiff's experts all along the line as to the cause of the fire and explosion.

After Mr. Schnidman testimony the defense rested.

After eight and a half days of testimony the opposing attorneys completed their summations and Judge Wheeler gave the case to the jury. It took the jury three hours to reach their decision in favor of the defendants. Attorney Perry Leary, with his associates H. Dutton Leary and Edwin W. Leary were congratulated by other attorneys and court room observers after the verdict was read. Clifford Searl, attorney for the plaintiffs reserved his right to make motions later to set aside the verdict.

As an interesting side note….A day after the fire a few interesting tidbits appeared in the paper. The first one concerned Cayuga Omibus Bus Company driver Alvin E. Hunter. It seems as Hunter had finished his last run of the night and was thinking of getting home he was passing the E.D. Clapp Company when a large explosion blew apart Scro's building sending large pieces of debris flying in all directions. One large piece of debris landed a few feet behind the bus Hunter was driving. It was a close call for if he had been driving any slower the debris would have landed on the bus' roof and injured Hunter. The second article concerned Jerry Madden, the man Police had taken to the hospital after he became overtaken by smoke inhalation. Mr. Madden reported that in his haste to escape the fire he lost $50.00. The paper reports the money was either left in his apartment or lost outside the burning building. A request was made for anyone that found the money to bring it to the paper so that it might be returned to Madden. The paper also noted barber Alphonso Passerello said it would be several days before he could open his barber shop. His father, Garlando, was busy cleaning up the mess in his small shoe repair shop located in the same building. Alphonso also stated that after the fire he returned to his home to collect a few belongings and found a large piece of debris laying across the bed where he and his wife had been sleeping. He said he felt as if they'd made a lucky escape.

CAYUGA COUNTY'S GANGSTER DEPUTY SHERIFF

In 1938, as the New York's governor's race between Democrat incumbent Herbert Lehman and Republican challenger Thomas E. Dewey heated up, Governor Lehman accused his opponent and the Republicans of hypocrisy, citing that a Republican Cayuga County Sheriff had appointed known gangster Arthur Flegenheimer (aka Dutch Schultz) as a deputy sheriff while the "Dutchman" was a fugitive from justice and under indictment. The speech was made at Morris High School in New York City. Dewey was a well known prosecutor who had taken on organized crime and the Dutchman in 1933. Obliviously, Governor Lehman was attempting to show that the Republicans, including Dewey, had been playing it both ways - taking a tuff anti-crime stance and prosecuting gangsters while consorting with them. Ironically, Lehman had appointed Dewey as a special prosecutor in New York County (Manhattan) to take on organized crime in 1935.

Sheriff Riley

Dutch Schultz

Gov. Herbert Lehmn

Thomas E. Dewey

When Lehman's accusation was published in just about every New York State newspaper, the local Cayuga County Republican leadership wasn't as surprised about the gangster deputy as most County residents. And when Dewey attempted to defend his comrades when he replied "that the Sheriff's political career ended when local Republicans found out about his appointment," his statement didn't douse the flames. Auburn Mayor Osborne replied "Dewey's statement will come with the same amusement to citizens generally as greeted the news that Dutch Schultz was one of our peace officers. Anyone who has followed local politics during the past five years will recall former Sheriff Earle Riley has been very much in evidence at Republican gatherings and party affairs especially in the primaries. Why he was seen at the local headquarters recently working very hard."

Finally, after all the back and forth publicity, former Cayuga County Sheriff Riley was pressured into explaining why he had appointed Dutch Schultz a deputy and given him a badge and handgun when he knew at the time his real name was Arthur Flegenheimer.

The former Sheriff told the press that he had received several complaints of illegal fishing at the head of the Owasco Lake at Cascade. That several men had been illegally netting fish, in that area, and he needed to put an end to it. That in August of 1933, a man who identified himself as Arthur Flegenheimer came into his office and told him that he was living at Cascade and could help him put an end to the illegal fishing if he was made a deputy. The former Sheriff stated that he later drove down to Cascade and found Arthur Flegenheimer registered at the hotel. He stated he believed that a stranger could work more effectively than a deputy who was well known, "so I appointed Flegenheirmer a deputy for the one purpose of stamping out the fish piracy in Owasco Lake."

Riley went on to say that at that time he had no knowledge that this man was the gangster Dutch Schutlz. "I did not know that until December 1933, when I saw a press dispatch regarding Dutch Schultz and the alias of Arthur Flegenheimer. I then did not know what to do. I considered hustling over to the County Clerk's office to cancel the appointment, but as I had only a few days left of my three year term I let the matter drop."

Riley went on to say that Flegenheimer did not make any arrests for game law violations and that he never saw him again after granting him the commission. He said that he had often granted appointments for deputy sheriffs for special work.

The Citizen-Advertiser newspaper, at the time, learned that Schultz had been a Deputy Sheriff in Hamilton County (NY), appointed to the position by Sheriff Beeker Wilson at Pleasant Lake in February 1933. The appointment was quickly rescinded when Sheriff Wilson was informed by NYSP that Flegenheimer was in fact the gangster Dutch Schultz. The paper reported that Schultz held his Cayuga County commission for more than sixteen months before it was rescinded.

Thus, Cayuga County for a short time employed known gangster Dutch Schultz as a Deputy Sheriff.

As some interesting side notes....Governor Lehman went on to defeat Thomas Dewey. Dewey continued his prosecution of gangsters including the Dutchman. In 1935, the Dutchman, close to an indictment, asked for the Mafia's permission to assassinate Dewey. The Mafia's Commission declined, but fearing that he would act on his own they ordered a hit on Schultz. He was gunned down at the Palace Chophouse, in Newark, NJ, on October 23, 1935.

Dewey running against Democrat John J. Bennett, won the NY Governorship in 1942. He later went on to run for President of the United States against both FDR and Truman losing both times. In one of the most famous headlines of the day the Chicago Daily Tribune printed, and sent to the streets, newspapers with the header "Dewey Defeats Truman."

R. THOMAS BURGER

I was really kind of intrigued when I learned that Dutch Schultz was carrying a badge. Why would a guy like Schultz want to be a Deputy Sheriff? So, I did a little research and I was quite surprised at what I found. It seems that in this era of gangsters, who were known to illegally carry weapons, it was to their advantage to carry a badge and many of them did. Being a sworn officer of the law it made legal for them to carry their "tools." It all makes sense now!

WE HAVE FOUND OUR NEW HOME

I saw fields and fields of grain
Stir'd by a breeze
Their stalks gently swayed
Like the waves
Of my home upon the sea
Lay anchor men, we have found our new home!

In the later part of June 1945, Mrs. George Underwood (nee Amy Louise Dunning), was sorting through her recently deceased brother David M. Dunning's papers when one caught her attention.

Written in her brother's hand, was a list of twenty-five Nantucket sea men who had immigrated to Auburn throughout the 1800s. According to legend the list was published, at Dunning's request, in 1885 by Frederick M. Coffin. Frederick Coffin was the son of Nantucket sea captain Joshua Coffin whose name appeared on the list as having arrived in Auburn in 1848. Frederick was also a distinguished Auburn artist and illustrator whose work appeared in several books and newspapers. He had also been employed by the Auburn Gaslight Company from 1873 to 1892.

It is believed Mr. Dunning compiled this list while several of these men were still alive for a presentation he was to make before the Historical Society. Here is a list of these "sea dogs" (most were listed as Captains) who drifted in from sea to make Auburn their new home:

1) Frederick Coffin (1827)
2) Jared Gardner (1827)
3) Thomas Bunker (1827)

4) William Swain (1827)
5) William Coffin (1827)
6) George Swain (1827)
7) Obed Folger (1827)
8) George Chase (1830)
9) Peter Fosdick (1830)
10) Henry Tracy (1833)
11) Thomas Hussey (1835)
12) Nathaniel Gorham (1835)
13) Thomas Folger (1835)
14) James Coffin (1835)
15) David Barney (1835)
16) Samuel Barney (1835)
17) Alex Marshall (1835)
18) Nathaniel Fitzgerald (1835)
19) George Crocker (1840)
20) Charles Coffin (1840)
21) Shahael Cottle (1844)
22) Joshua Coffin (1848)
23) Williams Downs (1850)
24) Frederick Myrick (1856)
25) Obed Hussey (1860)

What was it that made all these old veterans of the sea move to Auburn? It seems David Dunning had the answer.

What they told him was that their livelihood, that is whaling, was beginning to peter out. Because of the development of petroleum the whale's oil was no longer in high demand to light lamps.

Many of these sons of Nantucket were thrifty and of sterling stock. They brought their life savings with them and invested it in the homes they built, bought or enterprises they started. Captain Charles Coffin built his large home on west Genesee Street which was later converted into a large addition to the Genesee Street School. Captain George Chase was one of the original founders of the old Auburn Gas Company. Captain Thomas Hussey became prominent here through his invention of the Hussey mowing reaper. Captain William Swain settled on what later became the J. Reynolds Wait farm on Genesee Street. He later built a beautiful mansion at the corner Grover Street and Tuxill Square. After his death the house passed through other hands—the Perrys and later Henry D. Titus, the superintendent of the Southern Central RR. At one time the house belonged to Dorcas Tucker, the mother of former Auburn Doctor William Tucker. After they abandoned the property it fell on hard times and through the late 70s and early 80s it sat vacant and in disrepair. It was then bought and remodeled and was featured on HGTV.

Captain William Swain's home at 24 Grover Street

Some interesting side notes.....When Captain George Chase arrived in Auburn in 1830, he purchased a large tract of land on North Street that extended to State Street and build his home on North Street. On his property were stone quarries. Some of the stone from these quarries was used to build Auburn Prison. He was known as the ultimate entertainer and connoisseur who could spin a tale of his true life adventures at sea during an eloquent dinner he prepared. He was also served as the coroner when the Van Nest family was murdered.

Captain William Swain's father had been a Nantucket sea captain. However, William was born in Saratoga County, NY around the time of British General Burgoyue's surrender in 1777. As a child he undoubtedly had seen "red coats" near his father's home. After his family returned to Nantucket he joined a wealthy British shipping enterprise and eventually obtained the rank of Captain. On the open seas he once narrowly escaped a French-Man-Of War, suppressed a mutiny on his ship and he was responsible for sinking a French privateer that had attacked his ship even though his ship had but one cannon. He died in 1875 and is buried at St. Peter's Church, on Genesee Street.

ROBBERY SUSPECTS APPREHENDED QUICKLY

J. Earl Myers had worked the overnight shift at the YMCA front desk many times. Occasionally, a late night or early morning traveler would show up and need a room but most of his nights were long and quiet. He was never really concerned there would be any problems. However, on Tuesday morning July 17, 1951, his quiet morning was about to change.

At 4:50am, two young men entered the Y and used the men's room. When they reappeared they asked Myers if he had a room available. Myers told the two that all the rooms were taken but they could use the reading room for $1.00 each. The two sat on a bench for a while discussing it and then appeared about to leave when they turned around and approached Myers again. This time they yelled "This is a robbery!" When Myers looked to face the two he saw one was now pointing at shotgun at him while the other held a knife. They demanded all the cash in the register which Myers quickly handed over. They told him to put the money in a bag and he complied. The two then threatened Myers not to phone Police for ten minutes. As they were about to leave the younger male asked "What about your wallet," but was quickly quieted when the other male told him "Forget the wallet, let's get out of here." With that the two quickly ran out the front door and into the morning darkness. Myers immediately phoned the Police and informed Desk Sergeant Joe Ryan what had just happened. Police were quickly dispatched and an APD soon followed. Mr. Myers reported he'd turned $14.50 over to the bandits.

Meanwhile on the other side of town Officers Bob Randall and Mike Breanick, both men had just come on duty at 4:00am, were making their rounds along the Franklin Street area. At that time of the morning, particularly on a Tuesday morning, there weren't too many people or vehicles moving about. So when a car caught their attention they decided to run the plate number. When they received the data they learned that the car had been reported stolen from Syracuse earlier Monday.

As the two Officers pulled in behind the stolen car and hit the emergency red light their prey failed to pull over and began to speed up. As the two cars criss-crossed side streets they ended up on Grant Avenue and headed out of town. Officer Randall's first attempt to pull alongside and over take the stolen car failed. But his second attempt was successful. He forced the car to the curb and it came to an abrupt stop in front of 196 Grant Avenue, near the Coke-Cola  plant. The two Officers approached the car with guns drawn and ordered the two occupants out of the vehicle. They almost immediately realized the two young men matched the description of the young robbers. After securing their suspects, the Coppers searched the two and found one in possession of a pearl handled knife and the other had $12.65. A search of the vehicle revealed a loaded 12-gauge sawed-off shotgun under the front seat, and inside the glove box a YMCA money bag and two extra shotgun shells. The two were brought to Headquarters and turned over to Detective Beecher Flummerfelt. Earl Myers was brought to the station and quickly identified the two boys as the pair that robbed him and the recovered money bag.

The two young men, both from Genoa, were Donald Garrett, age 21, and Charles Shaw, age 20. Both were charged with Robbery 1st. Degree and Possession of a Weapon. They pled innocent at their arraignment later that morning before Judge John Naskiewicz and were sent to County Jail. In October, a Grand Jury upheld the charges and a trial date was set for early November.

On Friday November 2, 1951, Donald Garrett appeared in County Court before Judge Gerald Hewitt. He was represented by Auburn attorney Paul Mcgill. The people were represented by DA Theodore Coburn. At the hearing DA Coburn noted that in 1948 Garrett had been sentenced to Elmira Reformatory as a youthful offender. After a discussion with his attorney Garrett informed the Judge that he wanted to change his plea to guilty. The Court accepted his plead and sentenced Garrett to the Elmira Penitentiary. Charles Shaw faired much better as he was granted youthful offender status and referred to Probation Officer Elliot R. Wilkie.

As an interesting side note....Only four days after Officers Randall and Breanick were involved in the arrest of Garrett and Shaw they became involved in a high speed chase that ended when the suspect vehicle's tires were shot out. Around 5:00am, Friday morning July 20th., State Police from the Skaneateles office notified Auburn Police that Troopers John O'Malley and John Wilder were pursuing a stolen station wagon from Skaneateles into Auburn on Genesee Street. They reported the pursued vehicle was traveling in excess of 80mph and had been stolen from Ossining, NY. Near the East Genesee Street city limits Officers Randall and Breanick spotted the vehicle and took up pursuit with the State Police in tow.

With Police in close pursuit the car drove west on Genesee, continued onto Market Street, made a sharp right turn onto North Street and then a sharp left onto Garden Street.

As the vehicle sped by Police Headquarters, Sergeant Joe Ryan and Officer Joe Myers joined the pursuit. Attempts to overtake the car weren't successful. At one point Randall pulled alongside the car only to be sideswiped. Finally, on Garden Street, Officer Breanick fired four shots at the tires while Randall, using his left hand and steering with his right, fired several more shots at the fleeing vehicle. The driver of the stolen car swerved wildly, using the whole street, in an attempt to avoid the fired bullets. Near the intersection of Garden and State Streets it all came to an end when the driver lost control and struck the curb. The car came to a stop near the gas station on the corner.

MICHAEL W. BREANICK

The driver of the stolen car was identified as Gordon Hastie, age 24, formerly of New York City. He had stolen the car earlier Thursday from a driveway in Ossining. In Hamilton, NY, he gassed up and then drove off without paying. The State Police were alerted to the incident and later learned that the car had been reported as stolen. Troopers O'Malley and Wilder attempted to stop the vehicle in Skaneateles and had fired warning shots when the driver failed to comply. It was reported that not only had three of the vehicle's tires been shot out several other rounds had damaged the car's body. After Auburn Police issued Hastie several V&T tickets he was turned over to the State Police to answer charges in Hamilton and Ossining.

The paper made note that the whole incident began in a prison city and ended in a prison city, not far from the main gate. Auburn Police Chief Chester Bills stated a similar incident occurred fifteen years earlier when an escaped Ossining prisoner was apprehended near the Auburn prison gate.

THEY WERE HEROES

Shortly after the Revolutionary War settlers began a westward journey into the newly opened "frontier." Part of this vast new "frontier" would later become what is now Cayuga County and the City of Auburn. Militias were still needed and these settlers served willingly. Their distinguished service can be traced back to the War of 1812 through today's modern wars in Iraq and Afghanistan.

Although many of these men and women distinguished themselves, and many never made it home, many others earned Silver and Bronze stars and Purple Hearts. But only a few individuals born in Cayuga County earned a Medal of Honor. Some of these men had moved from the area by the time they received their Medal of Honor, but they were all born in Cayuga County. The next few pages will be dedicated to them and a few of my own personal heroes.

Charles L. Barrell was born in Conquest, on August 1, 1842. At a young age his family moved to Michigan. At the age of 20 he enlisted in Co. D, 17th. Michigan Infantry. He was promoted to Sergeant on January 3, 1863 and Second Lieutenant on October 29, 1863. He was reassigned to Co. C, 102nd. Colored Infantry Troops. A year later he was made a full Lieutenant. On April 17, 1865, near Camden, S.C., Union Colonel Henry Chipman was securing the area and under heavy Confederate fire. He sent Lt. Barrell with dispatches for General Potter. Lt. Barrell needed to cross enemy lines to deliver the messages. En-route to General Potter's position, Lt. Barrell captured an enemy orderly and with his assistance made his way around the enemies' positions to successfully deliver Chipman's dispatches. Returning to Chipman's position with re-enforcements on the 18th., Chipman was able to push forward driving the Confederates from their positions. Lt. Barrell received his Medal of Honor for bravely entering enemy positions and returning with the needed re-enforcements. He died in 1914 and is buried in Hooker's Cemetery, near Wayland, Michigan.

Kenyon's Stone and Medal of Honor Plaque, Lakeview Cemetery

Samuel P. Kenyon was born in Ira in1846. During the Civil War he served with Co. B, 24th. NY Cavalry. The regiment served in many battles, most notable The Wilderness, Spotsylvania Court House, the siege of Petersburg and the surrender of Lee's army at Appomattox Court House. At Sailor's Creek, Virginia, on April 6, 1865, his regiment along with the 10th. NY Cavalry, 1st. NJ Cavalry and 1st. Pa. Cavalry, charged the confederates under heavy fire. They broke the enemy's lines, capturing many prisoners and destroying a large Confederate wagon train. The heavy toll on Lee's army prompted Lee's despairing remark "My God, has the army dissolved?" The battle has been described as the death knell of the Confederacy. Private Kenyon was awarded the Medal of Honor for capturing an enemy's battle flag that day. He was mustered out of service as Quartermaster Sergeant and died in 1884. He is buried in Lakeview Cemetery, Richfield Springs, NY.

George Washington Thompson was born in Victory, in 1847. He enlisted as a private in the US Army in Syracuse, and was assigned to Co. C, 2nd. US Cavalry. He was sent to the western frontier to fight the Plains Indians. On May 15, 1870, he along with four other cavalrymen were searching for stray horses along the Little Blue River, in Nebraska, when they were ambushed by 50 hostile Indians. During a two hour fire fight the men killed three and wounded seven of the attackers before driving them off. With all of their horses killed the men withdrew but not before taking under their charge a settler's family of two women and one child. They succeed in returning to camp later that evening with only Private Thomas Hubbard wounded. On June 22, 1870, the five men received the Medal of Honor for "gallantry in action." As an interesting side note....nearly two years later, Private Thompson deserted but was apprehended a short time later. Only two months later he successfully deserted and disappeared forever from public record.

William W. Winegar, was born in Springport on October 20, 1844. He entered service there and was assigned to Co. B, 19th. NY Cavalry. During his service he held the ranks of Private, Corporal, Sergeant and Lieutenant. On April 4, 1865, at Five Forks, Va., Lt. Winegar was advancing ahead of his company when he was surrounded by several Confederates. He quickly accosted a nearby flag bearer and with one well placed shot demanded the Confederate unit to surrender. His action so demoralized the Confederate unit that they surrendered with their battle flag. On March 3, 1865 he was awarded the Medal of Honor. By the end of the war he had obtained the rank of Brevetted Captain. He resided in Bath, NY and died there on September 3, 1916. He is buried in Onondaga Cemetery, in Bath, NY.

Robert Styker was born in Auburn on November 9, 1944. He grew up in Throop and graduated from Port Byron High School. He enlisted in the US Army on January 22, 1963 and re-enlisted in 1965. While serving in the US Army near Loc Ninh, Vietnam, on November 7, 1967 his unit came under heavy enemy fire. Noticing that the enemy was attempting to surround his unit and cut if off from supporting units Spec. 4 Styker repeatedly launched his grenade launcher into enemy positions. While doing so he saw several wounded comrades in the "kill zone" of a claymore mine. Undaunted, Sec. 4 Styker pushed forward tripping the mine and absorbing its full impact when it exploded. His unselfish act saved the lives of six wounded comrades. His father Harold posthumously received Robert's Medal of Honor from Vice President Spiro Agnew in 1969. As an interesting side note....On February 27, 2002, the Army commissioned its new armor vehicle The Styker in Robert and Stuart (not related/MOH recipient/killed in WW2) Styker's honor. Styker Homes, in Auburn is named in his honor as well as the AmVet Post 513, in Montezuma. Robert is buried in Pine Hill Cemetery, Throop.

My personal heroes

John E. Burger is my uncle and is better known as "Otso" to his friends. He was born in Auburn in 1923. He was the son of Leona Sullivan Burger and resided on Park Place. He had a brother Robert "Butz," and a sister Marjorie. He enlisted in the US Army and served during WW 2 as a Private with Co. A, 81st Cavalry Recon Squadron (mechanized). On April 25, 1945, in the vicinity of Sisso, Italy, under heavy enemy fire, Private Burger and three others, with a light tank, succeeded in establishing a road block that held up the retreating enemy and allowed Allied planes "to cause serious damage to the enemy column." He was awarded a Bronze Star for his action. He married Lorraine Sanford and they resided on Mattie Street with their six children. He was a 38 year veteran of the Auburn Fire Department. He died in 1999 and is buried in St. Joseph's Cemetery.

Gerald (Jerry) Burger is my cousin and John's son. He was born in Auburn on Memorial Day 1949 and graduated from Central High School. He enlisted in the US Army in February 1967 and arrived in Vietnam in July of that year. On September 19th., he along with thirteen other members of the 196th. Light Infantry Brigade, were on a 20 day mission in the Quang Tri province in northern Vietnam. The unit came under enemy sniper fire every day. On the tenth day they encountered no opposition until they had set up camp for the night. The Viet Cong had snuck up to within 15 feet of the camp and opened up with small arms fire and grenades. Under intense enemy fire the men returned fire with everything they had except their machine gun. The men had set up camp in front of the gun emplacement making it useless. Private Burger moved forward to assist the men move the gun from its position. While doing so, he was struck with grenade shrapnel. The fire fight continued for another hour until the enemy withdrew. Of the 14 men in his unit three were killed and eight wounded. He was awarded a Purple Heart.

After a medical leave, Jerry returned to Vietnam and was assigned to Co. A, 4th. Bn., 12 Infantry. On May 30, 1969, his unit was on a reconnaissance operation near Saigon when they suddenly came under intense enemy fire from a well entrenched Viet Cong force. They immediately became pinned down. Private Burger moved forward under fire to take out an enemy position with a well placed hand grenade. He continued to expose himself to place more effective suppression fire upon the enemy, enabling two comrades to move forward and take out another enemy bunker. During the intense fire fight Private Burger received a painful wound but continued to bring effective return fire upon the enemy until the engagement was successfully concluded.

For his bravery he received a Bronze Star with Valor and another Purple Heart. Jerry resided in Fleming, was their Fire Chief for many years and has four daughters. He died in 2005 and is buried in St. Joseph's Cemetery with his wife Cindy near his father and mother. Jerry and I grew up together on Mattie Street and were very close. We shared a lot of great adventures and secrets. He died too young and is greatly missed.

Lance Cpl. John J. Rhodes

John J. Rhodes was born in Auburn on September 27, 1947. He and his family resided on Logan Street, and he attended Central High School. When John and I were kids we attended Seward School (on Swift Street), together and were great friends. I remember John always loved reading and talking about the Civil War. Generals U.S. Grant and Robert E. Lee were two of his heroes. He joined the Marine Corps shortly after high school and early in 1967 was sent to Vietnam. Lance Corporal Rhodes was assigned to H&S C0., 3rd. Bn., 9th. Marines. In October 1967, a jeep he was riding in became involved in an accident with a tank and John was killed. The accident happened in the Quang Tri area of South Vietnam. John was survived by his parents, two sisters and two brothers. He is buried at Soules Cemetery, in Sennett.

Donald J. Ryan was born in Auburn in 1948 and resided with his family on Camp Street. He attended Central High School, but as kids we were together at Seward School. He really didn't live too far from Mattie Street, so it was easy for him to participate in many of our big neighborhood baseball and football games and sliding down Vandenboush Ave.-- two or three on a sled was a must in the winter. Donald joined the Marine Corps in April 1966 and was assigned to Co. D, 1st. Bn., 9th. Marines. He was sent to Vietnam in December 1966. On March 14, 1967, Corporal Ryan was wounded in action and received a Purple Heart. Early in October 1967, Donald was killed in action near the Quang Tri area of South Vietnam. He was survived by his parents and two younger brothers. He is buried in St. Joseph Cemetery.

Ferdinand W. Glessing Jr. was born in Auburn in 1948. He resided with his family on Osborne Street and we attended Seward School together. After graduating from West High School, Fred joined the Marine Corps. He was a Lance Corporal and was killed in action near DaNang, South Vietnam, on January 3, 1968. He was survived by his mother, one brother and a sister. He is buried at Soules Cemetery, Sennett. This photo of Fred was taken in my side yard on Mattie St., in 1957.

Terry E. Toole was born in Auburn in 1947 and resided on Capitol Street with his family. He was a graduate of East High School. Although Terry didn't live near me or go to school with me, as a young kid we would play together when I visited my grandparents who lived next door to Terry on Capitol Street. Terry joined the US Army in November 1967. Spec. 4 Toole, was a squad leader and machine gunner assigned to Co. D, 2nd. Bn., 25th. Infantry. In early June 1969, he was killed in action near Cu Chi, in South Vietnam. He received his second Bronze Star and a second Purple Heart for his bravery that day. As an interesting side note....Terry was a former Purple Lancer and in 1969 The Lancers awarded their first ever Terry Toole Trophy to one of their outstanding members for that year. Terry is buried at Soules Cemetery, in Sennett.

My dad,
SSgt. Robert "Butz" Burger,
USMC, WW 2 and Korea

My grandfather,
Private Joseph M. McDonald,
US Army, WW 1

My uncle,
SSgt. Joseph E. McDonald,
USAF, Korea

My father-in-law,
Private Joseph "Jiggs",
US Army, WW 2

I would like to thank all the men and women of Auburn and Cayuga County for their unselfish dedication, sacrifice and service for our Country.

ONE TENANT DIES AS AUBURN HOTEL FIRE DESTROYS 100 YEAR OLD LANDMARK

Alarms and phone calls awoke Auburn Firefighters at 400am Friday morning July 3, 1970. Detailed to the corner of State and Clark Streets the arriving firemen found the Owasco Lounge, located on the corner at 13 State Street ablaze. Under the direction of Fire Chief William Maywalt the men quickly prepared to fight the growing inferno as tenants ran out of or jumped from the burning structure.

The building was somewhat of a local landmark having been built in 1877 and then known as the Louis Hotel (owner Louis Schuch). The building continued on as a hotel through many different owners with name changes over the years such as Schuch's Hotel, Beard's Hotel, Parker Hotel, The Majestic and finally in 1961 when it became Hotel Auburn, owned by John Alissandrello.

Raymond Flynn, manager of the hotel and lounge, stated that 20 of the 24 apartments in the upper four story building were occupied by 21 residents. Jimmy Martinez, an occupant of an apartment near the stairway to the second floor stated when he heard the fire alarm he opened his door and saw the stairway on fire. He said he grabbed a shirt, placed it over his head and ran down the stairs to the street.

As the firefighters fought the blaze many of the tenants were taken from the scene via ambulance to Auburn Memorial Hospital. Charles Boyce, age 67, was admitted for treatment of first and second degree burns. John Coughlin, age 53, was also admitted for severe smoke inhalation.

Several other tenants were treated and released. George Uzciko, no age given, and Frank Lissman, age 72, were treated for smoke inhalation. Albert McFall, age 42, suffered a back injury and Sergio Valentine, age 22, suffered a cut right hand and sprained ankle encountered after he was forced to jump from his second story apartment window. Other tenants escaped the building via a fire escape located on the west side of the building. A few were able to exit a Clark Street side door. By 500am several Red Cross and Salvation Army volunteers were at the scene to assist the displaced tenants and attend to the wants and needs of the firemen and police officers at the scene.

The firemen weren't immune to injuries either. Fireman Charles Barrette required 17 stitches for a cut hand. Lt. Bernie Searing punctured a foot after stepping on a nail and was given a tetanus shot and Lt. John Schiegel suffered two cut fingers. All were treated at Auburn Memorial Hospital and released.

It took firefighters three hours to extinguish the blaze before entry into the building could be made. Soon after the men began a search of the burnt out building they discovered one tenant hadn't made it out. Donald Bates, age 37, a lifelong Auburnian and Army veteran was found in his room on the third floor lying on the floor next to his bed. His body had been so charred that positive identification wasn't made until his dental records had been verified. He had been a resident at the hotel for about a month and had been employed at Auburn Plastics. Later newspaper editions noted that Mr. Bates was survived by two sons Russell and Donald and two daughters Kristine and Susan, his mother and two brothers. Funeral services were held at Heieck Funeral Home. Second Baptist Church assist pastor James Sheppard officiated. Burial will be at Soule's Cemetery.

Asst. Fire Chief George Bannon Jr. and Hotel/Lounge manager Ray Flynn both agreed that the building was a total loss. Although the cause of the fire has yet to be determined, Fire Chief Maywalt believes the fire started near a second story window, enabling it to race up the stairway where the flames burnt through an air shaft to the top floor. Auburn Police Detective Sergeant Carmen Bertonica was assigned to assist the fire department with its investigation of the fire and death. City officials report Bates' death was the first fatality in the City this year. There were five fire deaths in 1969.

Later that July the city building inspector condemned the building noting that the top two floors were unsafe and therefore unstable. AURA (Auburn Urban Renewal Agency) moved quickly to purchase the building and have it torn down. Today the area of this intersection and the block of buildings that ran along Clark Street, across from St. Mary's Church are part of the Loop Road and the Boyle Center parking lot.

As an interesting side note....Louis Schuch, the original builder and owner of the hotel was born in Laudau Rhein-pfals, Germany on March 6, 1829. He learned the hotel business from his father and worked at it for many years in Germany, France, Russia, Austria and Switzerland. He came to the United States in 1853 and quickly found work at a hotel in New York City. At one time he even worked aboard a steamship running between New York and New Orleans. In 1858 he was employed at the St. Louis Hotel, in New Orleans. By 1862 he was residing in Syracuse, NY. When the Civil War started he headed to New York City and was one of the first to enlist. He served with 20th. New York Turner Rifles. It is noted that the Turner Rifles were a German regiment that has quite a history of their own. Upon his discharge he came to Auburn and in 1864 married Madaline Keil, of Auburn.

Mr. Schuch's hotel at the corner of State and Clark Streets was conducted on the German plan and became a quite popular lay over and meeting place for locals. His thrifty, frugal and enterprising ways accumulated him a comfortable fortune. He is known by just about every Auburnian.

In early 1889, Mr. Schuch's health began to fail. He leased his hotel to James Beard and reserved a suite of rooms for his family. In the fall of that year he traveled to Mount Clemens, Michigan, in hopes the mineral springs located there would help restore his health.

On Sunday morning, March 6, 1892, he complained of chest pains on his left side and Doctor Creveling was called upon. After administering to Mr. Schuch nothing of a serious note was found. Mr. Schuch went to bed at 1000pm and at 1100pm his wife noted he was having difficulty breathing. Her attempts to arouse him were unsuccessful and Doctor Conway was called upon. By the time the doctor reached his bedside Mr. Schuch had died. Mr. Schuch was 63 years old and died on his birthday.

On Thursday March 10th, brief services officiated by Rev. George Feld, pastor of St. Lucas German Church, were held at the hotel and then at St. Peter's Church, with the Rev. Dr. Brainard officiating. Mr. Schuch was a member of the Crocker Post, Auburn City Lodge, Knights of Pythias, and Glee Club Germania. Members of each organization acted as pall bearers. Military honors were provided by the G.A.R. at Fort Hill Cemetery. He is survived by his wife and six children.

www.ingramcontent.com/pod-product-compliance
Lightning Source LLC
Chambersburg PA
CBHW050633160426
43194CB00010B/1648